"Susan challenges women to be true to themselves, to follow their passions, and to be honest about their strengths and weaknesses. This is no ordinary self-help book. Thanks to Susan, and the talented women she interviewed, the glass ceiling will cease to exist!"
—Janet Tiebout Hanson, president & CEO of Milestone Capital, and founder of 85 Broads

❧

"This book provides sound advice for women in the early stages of establishing a business career. I wish I'd read it earlier in my own! Many of these situations were familiar to me and I underlined several sections for sharing with junior associates (both women and men!) in my firm."
—Karen J. Curtin, executive vice president of Bank of America, N.A.

❧

"You'll be torn between keeping this book within easy reach and passing it along to your friends and colleagues."
—Benita Levy, managing director of Salomon Smith Barney

❧

"No matter where you are in your career, this book will help you gain an understanding of not only where you might want to go and how to get there, but also where you are and how you arrived there."
—Judy Freeman, partner at KPMG LLP

❧

"*The New Success Rules for Women* is a clear, concise primer that is designed to help women who are on the way up get there faster, smarter, and happier."
—Geri Brin, president of Brinsights, and producer of the Women & Co/FORTUNE conference

❧

"Women are achieving with a new style; one of grace and elegance, and combining it with feminine leadership. This book captures the true spirit of women who have succeeded in business."
—Michelle A. Rosen, department director at McDonald's Corporation

The New Success Rules *for* Women

The

New
Success
Rules *for*
Women

Susan L. Abrams

PRIMA PUBLISHING
3000 Lava Ridge Court · Roseville, California 95661
(800) 632-8676 · www.primalifestyles.com

PRIMA PUBLISHING and colophon are trademarks of Prima Communications Inc., registered with the United States Patent and Trademark Office.

All products mentioned in this book are trademarks of their respective companies.
"No, you're not too tough to suffer a Bout of Burnout"
reprinted with permission of Dow Jones & Co. Inc.,
conveyed through Copyright Clearance Center, Inc.

Library of Congress Cataloging-in-Publication Data
Abrams, Susan L.
     The new success rules for women : 10 surefire strategies for reaching your career goals / Susan L. Abrams.
     p.cm.
     ISBN 0-7615-2348-0
1. Women—United States—Psychology. 2. Women—United States—Life skills guides. 3. Women executives—United States—Psychology. 4. Women executives United States—Life skills guides. 5. Businesswomen—United States—Psychology. 6. Businesswomen—United States—Life skills guides.
7. Success. I. Title.
HQ1221.A25 2000
650'.1'082—dc21   00-027647
                                                    CIP

00 01 02 03 HH 10 9 8 7 6 5 4 3 2 1
Printed in the United States of America

How to Order
Single copies may be ordered from Prima Publishing, 3000 Lava Ridge Court, Roseville, CA 95661; telephone (800) 632-8676 ext. 4444. Quantity discounts are also available. On your letterhead, include information concerning the intended use of the books and the number of books you wish to purchase.

Visit us online at www.primalifestyles.com

To Billy, Andy, Jessica, and Caroline
for your inspiration, love, and support.

Contents

Leaders Interviewed

Acknowledgments ─────────────

A S YOU'LL SEE in this book, support systems are an important element of success for anyone. There are a great many people who are part of my support system and made *The New Success Rules for Women* possible. They include family, friends, colleagues, my agent, and the wonderful team at Prima.

And they include the 45 phenomenal women who are at the apex of their industries yet took time out to share their wisdom gained from many years of experience as they climbed corporate ladders and founded now-thriving businesses. Each of these women recognizes a profound obligation to help those who come behind them to rise up more effectively and efficiently, to shatter glass ceilings and walls, and to go as fast and as far as their dreams allow.

Thank you.

Introduction

A S WITH ANY rules, there are exceptions. The rules that follow were developed from my experiences and those of the female leaders profiled throughout this book. However, each woman brought to the table her own style, perceptions, and interpretations. And you must do the same.

There is power to sharing and efficiency in learning from others. I present to you in this book, concepts culled from years of experience by talented and determined women. Their lessons do not mitigate the value of your own personal experience, but perhaps, can help you get where you want to go a little faster and less painfully.

There also is comfort in knowing that you are not alone, though certainly, as these women have testified, it gets lonelier at the top. You are not alone in the issues you face and the challenges you encounter. And, you are not alone in not knowing all the answers. Each of these women recognized that they not only did not have, but did not need to have, all the answers. They just needed to recognize when and how to get help.

Don't be afraid to reach out and ask for advice. Both women and men are generally willing to share. That's what this book is all about. The individuals who have contributed generously their insights and experiences are sharing both what they learned from others and what they learned on their own.

They and I are trying to change the numbers, which indicate that while increasingly women are making it to the top, the progress is not fast enough. A recent Catalyst study found that just 11.2% of corporate executives and 2.7% of top earners at the Fortune 500 companies were women—in spite of the fact that women comprise 46% of the labor force. And, Catalyst projects that based on an average rate of change since 1995 when such data was first collected, women will occupy just 17% of Fortune 500 corporate officer positions in the year 2005.[1]

Therefore, it is imperative to learn from those who have "broken through" and achieved high levels of business success and to disseminate that knowledge to the many millions of working women who aspire to more. These women are searching for tools to improve their opportunities and positions. They want to know, given their own talents, how to go as far as they can. In short, they demand to know the rules for success.

---

1 Catalyst 1998 Survey of *Fortune* 500 companies.

The New Success Rules *for* Women

If You Like Music,
Work for Sony

POWER POINTER *Dare to be passionate about your job.*

Y OU WILL DO a great job at something you want to do. Whether it's a drive to instill a new corporate culture, an interest in improving the lives of children, or a desire to bring consumers "little moments of joy" through everyday products, today's business leaders are motivated by passion.

Passion is important to success. It doesn't matter what you do as long as you feel strongly about it. Passion makes the job at hand not only palatable, but also fun. It helps you stick with the job and take the long view through both the ups and the downs. And enthusiasm is contagious, so your passion becomes inspiration for others.

How do you find that passion within yourself and channel it to spark success? First, recognize its power to you as an individual and as a member of a team. Second, find the right job fit. And third, if you are not in your preferred job, begin positioning yourself to move to it gracefully.

The Power of Passion to Individual and Team Success

PASSION IS IMPORTANT to both individual and team achievement. Rose Marie Bravo's passion for her work has been critical to her success at all stages of her development. As a student, she enjoyed learning and studied all the time, taking the maximum number of credits while involved in a wide variety of clubs. Then, her first day in retailer Abraham & Strauss's executive training program, she thought to herself, "I love this. I can't believe this is work." Anything that had to do with work was okay. She couldn't get enough of it. Today, as chief executive of Burberry, Bravo still lives her job—as work and as a hobby. It gives her intellectual stimulation, financial reward, camaraderie, and self-esteem.

Passion is important to success. It doesn't matter what you do as long as you feel strongly about it.

Bravo is not alone in considering her work as both a career and a hobby. Many leaders I interviewed used the same phrase for describing how they viewed their jobs, and that's not surprising. The level of energy these leaders devote to their work is sustainable only when their employment is seen as more than just a job. At Chicago Children's Museum, my work was both a job and a hobby. I thought about it constantly, whether in the office or at home. I could not read a newspaper, visit a cultural institution, or hear about a new product without automatically considering potential partnerships, fund-raising ideas, or best practices that could be implemented at the museum. And that was before I had children. Once I did, an hour at the park or in a class with my kids also constituted an instant research forum. The line blurred between work and "play," but it was okay because it was fun. I was and remain today—as a board member—passionate about Chicago Children's Museum and its ability to positively impact the lives of children and their families.

Passion is contagious. Yours often will spread to those around you with motivational results. Deborah Borda's passion for music enabled her, as executive director of the New York Philharmonic, to be a highly effective leader. People responded to her intensity of feeling and commitment. Her enthusiasm spilled over, also, to her responsibilities as a fund-raiser. She notes, "I loved to ask people for money for the New York Philharmonic. It was an honor to ask and an honor to give." Following her arrival in 1991, Borda restored the New York Philharmonic's fiscal health through her financial savvy, product mastery, strong leadership, solid fund-raising, and passion.

VALERIE Salembier's enthusiasm for *Esquire* has helped her to increase the number of advertising pages in the magazine since she took over as publisher. Salembier, a voracious reader, grew up reading *Esquire,* which has a strong literary tradition. Therefore, when she visits advertising clients, her passion for the magazine becomes clear. This enthusiasm galvanizes advertisers, thereby translating Salembier's passion for her product into advertising sales dollars for her business.

Rose Marie Bravo

ROSE MARIE, THE oldest of two girls, was intense about achieving from a young age. Her drive carried her through school with flying colors, and she participated in many extracurricular activities. Rose Marie was not particularly athletic, however, so she did not engage in sports, sticking instead with what she was good at. She notes, "That strategy works in business, too. You need to know your strengths, and hire people to fill in your weaknesses. Find out what you don't know."

Following graduation from Fordham University with a BA in English in 1971, Rose Marie began her career in the executive training program at Abraham & Strauss, and that experience confirmed her passion for retailing. Rose Marie spent the next eighteen years at Macy's as part of a team that was like family to her. From 1987 to 1992, she was chairman and CEO of I. Magnin, the specialty division of R. H. Macy and Company. From 1992 to 1997, Rose Marie served as president of Saks Fifth Avenue and was a member of the board of directors of Saks Holdings, Inc. In 1997, she was named chief executive of Burberry, the British luxury goods company.

Rose Marie has been honored many times for excellence in retailing. She sits on the boards of Tiffany & Company and the National Italian American Foundation, and the advisory boards of both the Fashion Group International and the Fashion Institute of Technology.

Rose Marie is married and has two stepchildren.

Your team, too, will be motivated by your passion. When you care about something deeply, your excitement becomes palpable and leads others to want to share in it. Therefore, try to put yourself where you can be naturally enthusiastic. If you're not in that place, though, get beyond your own feelings in the short term while you work to find a better job fit. Take pride in doing your job well, even if you are unhappy. Your reputation as a strong performer will benefit you in the long run.

Find the Right Job Fit

FINDING A JOB that ignites your passion is critical. To do so takes thought, honesty, and self-awareness. There are many career counselors and books that can help, including the classic *What Color Is Your Parachute?* by Richard Nelson Bolles. Begin, however, by considering what you feel strongly about in all parts of your life. Are you a fitness enthusiast? Do you love animals? Do you have a special interest in helping battered women? In short, what gets you animated and excited? "If you like music, work for Sony. You can be an accountant for Sony as easily as for Citibank," counsels Tanya Mandor, an artist and an executive vice president at Revlon. Every day in her job for the cosmetics giant, Mandor works with color, shape, product, packaging, and advertising—all of which relate to her passion for art.

You need not be a professional musician to take advantage of your passion for music or an accomplished artist to pursue your passion for art in the workplace. You simply must find employment at a place in which your passion is important. After you have identified your passions, think about your functional interests and skills. Do you have an interest and the requisite skills (though those can be developed and packaged) in accounting, finance, advertising, human resources, marketing, or another area?

Stephanie Shern found her passion in the accounting field, although her first love was design. Shern made her own clothes through college, but could not draw. That fact plus the influence of her parents—her dad was an accountant and her mom had a business degree—swayed her to pursue a degree and a job in accounting. As it turns out, Shern particularly valued the opportunity that a large accounting firm afforded her to work in a variety of industries. She comments, "It's a great place for people in business to start if they are not certain what they want to do. I got to see different disciplines of accounting [tax, mergers and acquisitions, and more] and different industries." In her third year, Shern worked in the retail industry on a Saks Fifth Avenue project and particularly loved it. That experience confirmed her still strong interest in retail and led her to pursue accounting work in that field. Today, Shern is vice chairman and global director of the retail and consumer products practice at Ernst & Young.

FINDING THE RIGHT JOB FIT
TAKES EXPERIENCE

It may take trial and experience to figure out what is right for you. My first job out of college was at the investment bank Goldman Sachs. It built on my educational background in finance (and history) and my summer job experience in finance-related fields. While I learned a tremendous amount at Goldman, including the broad strokes of how many industries worked, what I found most interesting was an assignment that enabled me to travel through stores with the president of FAO Schwarz and discover what drives the retail toy business. I realized, through that experience, that running a business, rather than helping companies finance their businesses, was most interesting to me. Hence, I returned to business school intent on building my marketing and management skills as well as my knowledge of nonprofits, which, I thought, would be my long-term passion.

> *"If you like music, work for Sony. You can be an accountant for Sony as easily as for Citibank."*

After business school, I worked at McKinsey & Company, a management consulting company that gave me the opportunity to see a variety of businesses and the operations and strategic issues facing them. My heavy travel schedule, however, precluded me from expanding my exploration of the not-for-profit world, which had begun with consulting assignments during business school for Chicago's Museum of Contemporary Art and Northlight Theatre Company. I began to evaluate how I could combine my business interests with my personal interests in the nonprofit arena in areas related to children, education, and cultural institutions. My next job, vice president of marketing and strategic planning at Chicago Children's Museum, proved the perfect combination. For the first time, I was not only interested in what I was doing but also passionate about it. I could not and did not want to stop thinking about it, no matter what else I was doing. It was, in effect, both a job and a hobby. For close to six years, friends commented that they didn't know anyone who enjoyed their job as much as I did mine.

Elaine LaRoche

ELAINE AND HER younger brother grew up as first-generation Americans in a family that hailed from France and Haiti. She was always motivated by achievement and excellence. Elaine graduated as one of only a handful of women from the Georgetown School of Foreign Service in 1971. Although she passed both the Foreign Service and CIA exams, she turned down those opportunities, since she did not see many women at the top. Instead, she worked for Don Rumsfeld and then George Schultz in the Nixon White House. That early exposure to the highest levels of government taught her to think broadly, not just deeply, about organizations, processes, and how to have impact.

How did Elaine come to work for such high-level government officials right out of school? She responded to an ad for a French-speaking nanny and became the Rumsfeld family babysitter. Elaine and the Rumsfelds got along so well that they were happy to give her a head start in her career when an opportunity arose. However, following Watergate, Elaine became disillusioned with politics. She decided to pursue business, earned her MBA, and got a job at Morgan Stanley in institutional sales. Eventually, Elaine moved into the investment banking side of the business and rose to managing director.

Elaine currently lives in China and is CEO of China International Capital Corporation, a joint venture between Morgan Stanley and the China Construction Bank. She has three children.

Don't feel pressure to find the "perfect fit" immediately, particularly if you are just starting out. My jobs at Goldman Sachs and McKinsey had many pluses and some trade-offs. While they were not my "ultimate job," they each provided me with a terrific amount of growth and experience. I learned about many industries, strengthened strategic planning and problem-solving skills, and discovered more about myself and how, long-term, I wanted to spend my time. Often, one experience leads to another, so sticking with a job long enough to really understand it and do it well will pay dividends.

Elaine LaRoche spent a number of years in the institutional sales business at Morgan Stanley before realizing that she preferred the investment banking side. In order to make the change, LaRoche took short-term cuts in pay and seniority. And she took the risk to reinvent herself. She did not allow herself to be pigeon-holed in institutional sales, even though she had built her reputation and expertise in that area. Although LaRoche didn't anticipate it at the time, having experience on two sides of the business helped her, down the road, reach the upper echelon of management at Morgan Stanley. Don't be "shy" about new experiences. If you are inclined to try something new, be willing to go after it. Make it happen.

Recognize that everyone pays their dues and that there is no such thing as an entirely glamorous job. At Goldman Sachs and McKinsey, as a relatively junior employee, I got to work with senior executives at a host of interesting companies—helping them to solve problems and tackle issues of primary importance to their businesses. However, I also had to develop complex financial models and run varied business scenarios—over and over—often into the early hours of the morning. Even world travel, which sounds like a fabulous perk, becomes an exhausting experience when you are juggling time zones, jet lag, and job responsibility, not to mention outside commitments. Rose Marie Bravo maintains two offices as chief executive of Burberry—one in London and one in New York City. Consider that the next time you are dragged down by your commute. And remember, every job, like every aspect of life, involves trade-offs.

Recognize That Each Person's "Fit" Is Different

Each person has unique talents and interests, so each job match will be different. Everything that Phyllis Apelbaum is passionate about feeds her need to help people who come from backgrounds similar to hers—one of extreme poverty and limited education. Now, as chairman and chief executive officer of Arrow Messenger Service, she employs hundreds of such people as messengers in her delivery company.

How did Lillian Kraemer discover her passion for law? In a Russian history class in college, Kraemer found herself captivated by a paper comparing Russian and Western legal systems. At age eighteen, Kraemer embraced her inkling that law was right for her and, as she learned more, never wavered. From her limited original legal experience forward, Kraemer confirmed her passion for helping people to reach a goal or to solve a dispute through legal counsel, and she rose to become a senior partner at the Simpson Thacher & Bartlett law firm.

Try to be as specific as possible in identifying what ignites your passion. Is it making movies? Or, is it making movies in your own company? Or, is it making movies with certain partners? Or, is it making movies about certain subjects? The more you understand about what excites you, the better your chance of finding the right job fit. Following Lillian Kraemer's first exposure to law in her history class, she surmised that her passion was grounded in an intellectual interest. In law school, however, Kraemer realized her interests weren't scholarly; she desired to practice law. She was passionate not about legal issues in the abstract but about those circumstances that involved a client. Therefore, for Kraemer, teaching law, even though it was the right field, would not have made her passionate.

What motivates one person may not even be interesting to another. On the same day that I interviewed Stephanie Shern for this book, I also interviewed Dawn Mello, then president of Bergdorf Goodman

BRENDA Barnes, acting president and chief operating officer of Starwood Hotels & Resorts, has discovered her passion for two things: product and process. The common theme that motivates Barnes with all her jobs is that the product she promotes brings consumers some level of happiness. The products include sporting goods (Wilson); snack products (Frito-Lay); soft drinks (Pepsi); and a comfortable night's lodging (Starwood). Barnes also discovered she had a passion for process. At Pepsi, she labored to create a culture in which (a) customers came first and (b) every employee mattered. She loved her colleagues and the process of working to ensure that they and Pepsi's customers were highly valued.

Lillian Kraemer

LILLIAN, AN ONLY child, was born in Brooklyn in 1940. Family legend has it that when her mom woke up in the hospital after Lillian was born, she said to her husband, "I'm sorry. I know you wanted a boy." Her father, the story goes, replied, "Don't worry. It won't make a difference." And it didn't.

Lillian's parents, neither of whom went to college, imbued in her the expectation that she would make something of herself—on her own—and that life was something she should take charge of.

Lillian was a Phi Beta Kappa graduate from Swarthmore College in 1961. In 1964, she earned her JD with distinction from the University of Chicago, where she was a managing editor of the Law Review and elected to the Order of the Coif. Lillian became a partner at Simpson Thacher & Bartlett in 1974, concentrating in international securities and banking law before heading the firm's bankruptcy practice. Lillian, who retired from Simpson Thacher & Bartlett in 2000, is a fellow of the American College of Bankruptcy, a member of the Association of the Bar of the City of New York, a member of the Council on Foreign Relations, a director of the Lawyers Alliance for New York, and a member of the board of managers of Swarthmore College.

Lillian was married briefly and has no children, but she delights in spending time with her godchildren.

department store. First Shern, a vice chairman at Ernst & Young, cited her passion for the variety of clients and issues she encounters in her consulting work as a reason for her success. In a separate interview, Dawn Mello exclaimed, "Retail, that excites me to get up every day and want to come to work." As you can see, while in different fields, these women are united by a passion for what they do.

The more you understand about what excites you, the better your chance of finding the right job fit.

LET PEOPLE KNOW WHERE YOU WANT TO GO

When you see an opportunity you would like to go after, let people know. That way, they can help you achieve your objective. On the other hand, if your boss doesn't think it's possible at your company, she can inform you. With that information, you can adjust your plan or move on to reach your goal elsewhere.

A persistent "ask" helped Jane Thompson to achieve her goal to run a business. Thompson left McKinsey, where she was a partner, to pursue that goal at Sears. While she started in strategic planning, Thompson expected to "have a business" within two years. After three, she became more vocal. Just as she was considering leaving, Arthur Martinez was hired as chief executive officer to effect a turnaround. In Thompson's first meeting with Martinez, he said, "So, I hear you want to run a business." Thompson stayed in the strategy group to help engineer Sears' recovery, and then ran a succession of businesses: Credit, Home Services, and Sears Direct. It's important to let people know what you want to do so that they can help you achieve your objectives.

Decide to Move On If You Don't Love Your Job

THE bottom line regarding finding the right job fit is thoughtfully stated by Robin Foote, managing director of Randolph Partners: "Be true to yourself. Know what you want to do and be at peace with that. Be clear about what you can offer an organization and what you want in return. Find a place where what you are good at aligns with what the organization needs. Don't try to change yourself to conform to what you think others want or what you think you should be. Know yourself, be yourself, and use your energy to bring your dreams to life in an environment in which you are comfortable."

WHILE YOU DON'T always have the luxury to love what you do or get out immediately, it is an objective to work toward. Financial and other constraints may preclude leaving a job quickly; however, keep searching for employment that you will enjoy. As we all know, a job takes a lot of hours each day. So not only will you be more successful if you have something you enjoy and are passionate about but you'll also have more fun and be happier.

How do you know when it's time to leave a job? Making this decision is sometimes not as easy as it sounds. There's certainly comfort in the familiar, even when you know your job is not quite right. Moving on to a new situation involves taking risks and overcoming the inertia that often keeps us someplace—whether in a job, a relationship, or elsewhere—longer than we should stay.

Marilyn Lederer, chief operating officer at The CHEST Foundation, has four standards that she reviews to help her know when it's time to go. They can help you, too.

It's time to go when:

1. You are maintaining, not innovating.
2. The job becomes routine, and there's no real excitement to get out of bed for the day's challenges.
3. The challenge of the hunt or game fades.
4. Your old enthusiasm and sense of humor are not there.

Other signs it may be time to leave include (1) finding you are no longer learning as quickly as you would like, or at all, and (2) finding you have reached a plateau within your organization—such as when you and those for whom you work do not see avenues for advancement open to you. These criteria assume that you are driven to climb the ladder. If that is not your objective, then your criteria for moving on will be different. For example, if a comfortable job with colleagues you enjoy is what makes you happy, then recognize and seek that type of position. Your rate of learning and advancement may be less important to you. When you find the position that's right for you, try to excel and enjoy. It's okay not to want to be number one.

Being honest with yourself about who you are and what you like and dislike is critical in determining when to move on from a company or position. So, too, is an honest assessment of your skill set and the capabilities valued by the organization you are employed by or are considering a relationship with. For several years, Sheri Wilson-Gray worked at Procter & Gamble, where a quantitative orientation was valued. She looked around and saw colleagues who could "practically run regressions in their heads." That was not Wilson-Gray's strength, and one day a light bulb went off, saying, go somewhere where quantitative skills are not so critical, but where qualitative factors are. Her honest assessment of both her skill set and those qualities valued by her employer enabled Wilson-Gray to move forward to find a better opportunity for herself. Seek to garden where your seed can grow.

As we saw earlier, you may need to try more than once to find the optimal job fit. During the course of her career, Wilson-Gray has worked at Procter & Gamble, Playtex, Cheseborough-Pond's, Monet Jewelers, and Victoria Creations before settling in at Saks Fifth Avenue, where she has been for the last eight years and is now an executive vice president. Based on her own experience, Wilson-Gray recommends that you think through the following issues when you are frustrated and suspect it may be time for a change:

- What do I like about my job, and what do I dislike?
- What can I do to make the "likes" greater and the "dislikes" less?

Move On to New Opportunities Gracefully

WHEN IT'S TIME to go, plan your strategy carefully to maximize your chances of maintaining positive relationships with your colleagues, bosses, and employees. Once you have made your decision, you may feel the natural urge to run in and "unburden yourself" to your boss regarding your desire to leave. Avoid it. Instead, anticipate the issues and questions that will be raised by your boss, and plan your responses accordingly.

Here are some issues to consider:

- How much notice can you provide?
- What are your key responsibilities and projects that will need to be covered?
- Who do you suggest can handle them?
- What is needed to drive your projects to completion?
- Can you assist in the smooth transition of your responsibilities to others who will cover them in the short term or to someone who will take over your job?
- If someone will replace you, do you have any suggestions for hiring and training that person?

Additionally, be prepared for questions regarding why you are leaving and where you are going.

How you communicate your resignation has an impact on whether you will be able to maintain positive relations with colleagues at your soon-to-be former employer. Structure your notice as a conversation in which you inform regarding your desire to leave the company. Present a "positive spin" on why it is actually great for everyone, and make your departure as nonthreatening as possible. If you are leaving for the competition, that's a bit harder. If you are not, highlight that point and show how, perhaps, you might even be helpful in the future. In summary, "market" the fact that

Sheri Wilson-Gray

FOR SHERI, THE middle child of three girls, her parents were the most important people in her upbringing. They were loving and intelligent and made her feel like she could do anything.

Although Sheri did not participate in sports growing up, her daughter is an active participant. Sheri believes sports are a metaphor for life and teach key lessons: (1) don't take things personally; (2) don't be emotional and don't cry; (3) be a good sport; and (4) team work is important.

Sheri earned a BS in fashion retailing from Purdue University in 1972 and an MS in management from the Krannert School of Management at Purdue University in 1974. After graduation, she worked from 1975–1979 at Procter & Gamble, rising from brand assistant to brand manager. Sheri then served as marketing manager at International Playtex for two years and then as marketing manager at Cheseborough-Pond's from 1980 to 1983. Sheri began at Monet Jewelers in 1983 as director of marketing and by the time she left in 1990, she was vice president and general manager of the Monet Ventures Group. After a 1990–1991 stint at Victoria Creations as vice president, Sheri joined Saks Fifth Avenue in 1991 as vice president, marketing and advertising. In 1994 she was promoted to senior vice president overseeing marketing, advertising, public relations and special events, and in 1997 Sheri was named executive vice president.

Sheri is married and has two children.

you are leaving, and as in all your work, show your thoughtfulness and diligence.

The quality of your work, including your ethical standards, during your employment affects directly your ability to maintain future relationships. If people know they can count on you and you do a great job, then they will be more interested in keeping the connection.

The key is to make every effort to maintain an ongoing relationship rather than to burn bridges. Not only might you need references in the future, but there may also be opportunities down the road for business together or other collaborations. Therefore, clearly state that you've valued your experience at XYZ and that you'd like to leave the door open to future conversations and relationships. The best I've ever seen at maintaining positive relationships with former employers is Jim Harris, a partner at Z Group. He recently left Allied Riser Communications (ARC), where he had been chief marketing officer and regularly shuttled back and forth between its Dallas headquarters and his Chicago home. The company was progressing toward an initial public offering (IPO), and everyone was working intensely.

How did Harris gracefully leave ARC in order to work with Sergio Zyman at Z Group, while not only maintaining his relationships but also having ARC become a significant client? First, Harris proved his work efficacy and abilities while at ARC. He did excellent work—and lots of it. He could be counted on. Second, he left at a time that made sense for ARC—before the IPO books were compiled rather than after, or after the IPO itself. Third, he helped his employer to understand his motive. When he left ARC, its CEO understood that one of the world's leading brand marketers wanted him to be a partner in the business. And fourth, he offered to remain a resource for the company. In fact, his new role as consultant played to both his strengths and ARC's needs.

The bottom line: Work to prevent your employer from feeling as though it is losing. Turn the circumstances into as much of a win-win situation as possible.

🍩 POWER POINTER *Dare to be passionate about your job. For centuries, women have been passionate about their family life and other causes. Historically, when women worked, it was to support a family, not because they loved their jobs. It is only recently that women are becoming comfortable in asserting themselves as professionals. Now, women must find and pursue what they are passionate about in the work world. You will work harder yet smarter, have more fun, and achieve greater success with the right job fit. Dare to find employment in a field about which you are passionate.*

CHAPTER ONE SUMMARY AT-A-GLANCE

Use the checklist below to make sure you understand the points and steps discussed in chapter one.

Recognize the power of passion to individual and team success.

- ☑ View your work as both a job and a hobby.
- ☑ Motivate others with your passion.
- ☑ Put yourself where you can be naturally enthusiastic, or show an enthusiastic front until you can reposition yourself.

Find the right job fit.

- ☑ Determine what you are passionate about.
- ☑ Recognize your strengths and find an employer that values them.
- ☑ Don't feel pressure to find the "perfect fit" immediately.
- ☑ Realize that what motivates one person may not even be interesting to another.
- ☑ Let people know where you want to go.

Decide to move on if you don't love your job.

- ☑ Employ objective criteria to know when to go.
- ☑ Learn more about yourself through experience.

Move on to new opportunities gracefully.

- ☑ Plan your departure strategy to maximize your chances of maintaining relationships.
- ☑ "Market" your decision to leave.
- ☑ Keep the door open to future conversations and relationships.

Keep Your Eye on the Ball

⤵ POWER POINTER *Put the right support network in place to maximize your focus and flexibility.*

FOCUS, FOCUS, FOCUS. Those are the only words I've jotted down in preparation for this interview," quipped Dawn Mello when I talked to her.

What are today's leaders focusing on? Primarily two things: (1) doing the best they can in the job at hand, and (2) their goals. For some the goals are immediate, while for others, they are longer-term, far-reaching beacons that guide them. All, however, agree that you must not let your goals blind you to opportunity. Instead, learn to take advantage of interesting opportunities while keeping your eye on the ball.

Your professional career will have ups and downs, times of great progress and other periods when you feel stuck in a quagmire. In each of these periods, maintain your focus on both the job at hand and on your ultimate goal. This focus will help you learn from your situation, accomplish what you set out to do, and progress to the next level.

Focus on Doing the Best You Can at Your Current Job

A FOCUS ON excelling in your current job always helps you succeed. Colleen Barrett was interested in law but couldn't afford law school, so she attended legal secretarial school and worked summers to achieve her two-year bachelor degree. Her goal was to be the best legal secretary to her boss, Herb Kelleher. She succeeded so well in that job that Kelleher brought Barrett with him when he founded Southwest Airlines. As she continued to excel, Kelleher increased her responsibility until she became executive vice president of customers at Southwest and the most senior woman in the airline industry. Barrett notes, "I focus on where I am today and where I want to be tomorrow. Even today, my goals are more project-oriented. I am not a career-path planner."

While most successful people keep an eye on a distant goal, they all stay focused on the job at hand. In a highly competitive world, if you are not focused on excelling, then someone else will preempt you at whatever you are doing. Whether or not you love your current position, excelling at your job ultimately will help you move forward to the next opportunity. When Rose Marie Bravo was a perfume buyer at Macy's, her immediate objective was to create the best array of perfumes in the marketplace. The rewards and promotions that followed were the natural result of a job well done. Bravo never set as a goal, for example, to be president of Macy's. Instead, she committed herself to excellence and followed the path as it became clear.

Colleen Barrett

COLLEEN GREW UP in a poor family as the oldest of three children—she had two younger brothers. Although they had little money, she learned generosity from her mom, who showed her that there was always room for an extra plate at the table. Her mother also "hounded into her" that there was nothing Colleen couldn't do if she set her mind to it.

Colleen's only professional interest was in the law, as she had an uncle who was a lawyer. Since she couldn't afford law school, she attended legal secretarial school and worked summers to earn a two-year bachelor degree. Following graduation, Barrett worked as a legal secretary for Herb Kelleher, and when he founded Southwest Airlines, Barrett became his executive assistant. Colleen notes, "I was a darn-good secretary and loved it. With the right partner, you can learn and be part of so many things." Since then, she has climbed the ladder at Southwest—including positions as vice president of administration and currently executive vice president of customers and as such, oversees all internal and external communications. Colleen is the airline industry's most senior woman.

Colleen is divorced and has one son.

Kitty D'Alessio aspired to be the best she could be at whatever she was doing—whether it was a school assignment, an extracurricular activity, or a dinner party. In the professional realm, if she was making an advertising pitch at Revlon, then she wanted founder Charles Revson to like it. If she made a new business pitch, then she passionately wanted to win the account. By focusing on success in her current project, she rose to become president of Chanel, president and chief executive officer of Carolyne Roehm, and, later, president and chief operating officer of Natori. Foster that same drive in yourself, and it will help you to achieve your goals. Remember the old adage, "If it's worth doing, it is worth doing well."

Whether or not you create a personal mission statement, goals will help you to achieve in both business and life.

Focus on Goals That Can Guide You

WHILE DOING YOUR best at your current job, keep in mind larger goals regarding your career and your life. A long-term, broad perspective has two distinct advantages. First, macro goals serve as a beacon, guiding you in the direction you desire to go. Second, they keep you from getting too caught up in smaller day-to-day issues. Essentially, they help you to keep perspective regarding what is truly important. Whether or not you create a personal mission statement, goals will help you to achieve in both business and life.

However, don't be so wedded to your goals that you miss opportunities. Instead, when it comes to both long-term, visionary goals and immediate, tactical goals, strive to remain flexible.

Does it matter if you prefer smaller, more incremental goals or longer-term, stretch goals? No. It's only important to choose a style of goal-setting that is comfortable for you. Some people are motivated by deadlines, while others are paralyzed by them. For some, a big goal is a strong impetus for accomplishment, while for others, commitment to a large objective is overwhelming. Below, I present how some of today's most successful female leaders use goals. Cherry-pick from them what feels right for you. As you'll see, some of today's leading executives have changed their style over time. You may, too.

Stretch Goals Can Serve as Beacons

If you are comfortable thinking big, then a long-term, stretch goal can assist you in achieving lofty objectives. As we've seen, Jane Thompson's clear goal to run a business enabled her to leave a successful consulting career and partnership at McKinsey to work at Sears. Similarly, Paula Sneed sets huge, seemingly unobtainable dream goals—personal and professional—that serve as beacons. Sneed notes, "You may do well without that beacon when things are going well, but it's harder in difficult periods without big goals. And, after you set your goals, you need a plan and hard work to get there." Before Sneed married, she sat down with her fiancé, who was graduating from MIT and also had large goals, and they did a joint time-line and plan. This road map not only showed them how they were doing over time but helped them to see that they had to make compromises for each other in order to both succeed.

After reading an article, in the early 1990s, regarding how few women there are on corporate boards, Sneed said to her husband and daughter, "That's my next goal." At the time, it seemed a stretch, as she had no clue how to go about it and was not receiving calls from executive search firms. However, the objective seemed reasonable, as Sneed believed that board service would enhance her professional growth and that she could contribute to another company's success. After she articulated her goal, Sneed considered what it would take to accomplish her objective. She concluded that she needed to be more senior in her own company and to have a strong reputation for the value of her counsel. Therefore, Sneed's new objective and insights motivated her to work harder and smarter at her job at Kraft and to expand her horizons within and outside of the company. As the years passed, she earned promotions and hit the radar screens of those doing board searches. She now serves on several corporate boards.

Deborah Borda's big goal was to lead a major symphony orchestra. While her initial goal was simply to work at a major symphony orchestra, once she achieved that, she knew she wanted the executive position. It felt right to her. Knowing that about herself enabled her to be strategic about accomplishing her goal, allowing her to focus on the steps she could take to achieve it.

USING INCREMENTAL GOALS

Incremental goals are more achievable than macro goals and also may increase the chance that you will be open to new opportunities as they arise. If your path is not too narrowly defined, then you won't worry about stepping off. And, setting achievable goals will build your confidence and keep you going.

Cynthia Round, former senior partner at Ogilvy & Mather and now a brand consultant, selects goals that she can "see on the horizon." In her first two months at college, she set a goal

Setting achievable goals will build your confidence and keep you going.

to be named one of the top ten freshman women at a school of twenty-three thousand, which she achieved primarily through leadership positions. Then, once she had achieved a 4.0 grade point average her freshman year, Round decided to do it for the rest of her college years. These immediate goals served as effective guideposts and motivators for Round as she progressed through school and her career. For some people, as for Round, incremental goals are the most comfortable.

To many who have achieved tremendous success, their current positions were inconceivable to them just a short while back. It is always feasible and desirable, however, to look toward the next level. That should never be out of reach, or you are in the wrong place. And after achieving a few "next levels," you'll find you really are senior within your organization. As a young woman, Janet Gurwitch Bristow didn't think about working her way to the top. In fact, when she began her career in the 1970s, no one thought of women running businesses. But Gurwitch Bristow looked at the next level and thought, "I can do that." Then, as she advanced, her confidence, her knowledge of herself and the world, and her vision were enhanced, so that she was able to see further. It was not until Gurwitch Bristow became a senior vice president at Foley's that she realized she could and would like to run a company. Today, she is chief executive officer of Gurwitch Bristow Products, the manufacturer and marketer of Laura Mercier Cosmetics.

Stephanie Shern also focuses intently on goals that she can see on the horizon. After a couple of years at Arthur Young, when Shern realized that she not only liked what she did but was good at it, she set for herself the goal of becoming a partner—which she subsequently achieved. After Shern made partner, she set the goal to become a "player" in the newly merged Ernst & Young firm. Therefore, rather than maintain her previous role, which would have been less risky, she instead sought new roles in the combined entity. Through her efforts, she ultimately became vice chairman and a member of the combined firm's management committee.

A "project orientation" is consistent with setting incremental goals. Nancy Karch, a former senior partner who ran McKinsey & Company's Atlanta office, and Sharon Patrick, a former McKinsey partner who is president of Martha Stewart Living Omnimedia, share an interest in completing interesting projects. They do not set visionary goals for themselves. Karch comments, "I am a path rather than an end-point person. I get interested in things and then want to get them done." Karch, for example, stumbled into business school and then consulting "for a few years." As interesting projects and challenges presented themselves, Karch stayed with them and "followed the trail." Similarly, Patrick thinks about a "body of work"—which translated into assignments at McKinsey and at other jobs once she left—versus a title or specific career goals and tracks.

Lillian Kraemer discovered in college that she wanted to be a lawyer, but she commented "absolutely not" when I

Stephanie Shern

STEPHANIE WAS BORN in 1948 in a small town in Pennsylvania, and her younger sister is Mary Ann Domuracki, who is also profiled in this book. Although Stephanie's first love was design and she made her own clothes through college, her business-oriented family (her dad was an accountant and her mom had a business degree) directed her toward a profession. Therefore, she took marketing classes and earned an accounting degree from Penn State. After graduation, Stephanie interviewed with what were then the Big Eight accounting firms because, due to their size, the opportunities were greater.

Stephanie found her fit at Ernst & Young, where she has spent her entire professional career and where she treasures the wide variety of issues and clients she encounters. During her more than twenty-five years at the firm, Stephanie has risen through the ranks to become partner and then vice chairman. She is global director of the retail and consumer products practice at Ernst & Young and a member of its management committee. Stephanie speaks frequently at industry events and schools. She is a member of several industry groups and contributes to business and trade publications such as the *New York Times,* the *Wall Street Journal,* and *Women's Wear Daily.*

Stephanie and her husband are avid Francophiles and love to travel together.

asked her if she had a long-range plan. She elaborated, "I hope I don't know what I'll be doing in two years. And I hope I'm imbued with enough passion to reach out for whatever comes." Kraemer is one of the country's leading bankruptcy attorneys, but it is a specialty she fell into. In 1977, she wrote the loan agreements between Chrysler and its banks. Then, when Chrysler faced financial difficulty shortly thereafter, it was Kraemer who spent two years helping them work through their troubles. She could have viewed that experience as a two-year sidetrack from her banking practice. Instead, Kraemer recognized a new level of passion for helping clients fix problems, and she seized the opportunity. She set up a bankruptcy practice and a department that didn't exist, and then built a national reputation and business in bankruptcy law.

EMPLOYING A MILESTONE APPROACH

A milestone approach combines a big goal with incremental objectives. If you say, as did Connie Duckworth, that you want to run a business one day, but remain flexible about which business and precisely how you'll get there, you'll have a greater chance of success. Duckworth set that one large goal, and then used smaller goals along the way to help reach it. For Duckworth, the short-term goals are more tactical. Her objective might be to win a certain piece of business, develop a new client relationship, or undertake a new business initiative. These tactical goals have discreet start and end points. As Duckworth accomplishes these near-term objectives, or milestones, she moves closer to realizing her stretch goal.

Brenda Barnes also successfully employs a milestone

strategy. From the time Barnes worked at a flower shop while still in school, she realized, through her strong desire to grow and improve the enterprise, that one day she wanted to run a business. Instead of intricately plotting all the steps she anticipated, she tried to keep herself moving in the right direction. As a product manager at Wilson Sporting Goods, she thought, "If I keep going, I should get to vice president of marketing at this salary and time. And then, I'll get sales experience. . . ." After she set her milestones, she focused on gaining appropriate experience and excelling in the job at hand, and she found that the rest usually took care of itself.

Tailor Your Own Approach to Goal-Setting

IF YOU ARE uncomfortable with a particular style of goal-setting, then change it. Goals should be tools to facilitate your success and happiness. They should not become constraints or threats that cause additional angst. You already experience enough pressure from the job and from within, so don't hold yourself to a goal or strategy that isn't right for you.

Phyllis Apelbaum has adapted her approach to goal-setting to meet her needs over time. She is, by nature, extremely goal-oriented and likes to know going into a situation what end result she's seeking. In her younger days, Apelbaum set virtually unobtainable stretch goals and then used to push herself until she was ragged trying to achieve them. She no longer does that. Now, she employs a more strategic approach to setting goals. Following is the checklist she now employs to guide her in setting appropriate goals. The point, though, is that if one approach isn't working, change it.

Phyllis Apelbaum's Guide to Goal-Setting
- Is it reasonable?
- What will it take to get there?
- Are the resources available?
- What will you do when you get there?

To Write or Not to Write?

Whether you commit your goals to paper or keep them in your head is a personal decision. At least initially, however, it's helpful to write out your thoughts. This exercise forces you to organize your thinking, and having a written document facilitates periodic review.

Just as it is imperative to have a plan when running a business, so, too, is it advisable for you to have a plan for managing your career. It's natural to extend goal-setting to your own personal development. Janet Gurwitch Bristow finds that setting down clear goals provides her with a road map, ensuring that she won't get lost. And it has emboldened her to communicate her objectives to her bosses. When you communicate your objectives to your superiors, if they value your role, they can work with you to help you succeed. Equally important, if they don't think your

Goals should be tools to facilitate your success and happiness. They should not become constraints or threats that cause additional angst.

expectations are reasonable, they can let you know so you can make other decisions and plan accordingly. To maximize your benefits from planning, it is helpful to look four to five years into the future.

To Get Personal or Not?

Including personal goals along with your career plans adds another level of benefit. Combining your professional and personal objectives pushes you to consider both aspects of your life and their relative importance to you. Additionally, you'll see whether you are being realistic in each area. For example, if you aspire to add a major new work-related responsibility, it may not be the year to add demanding new community activities. At the start of each year, Carole Black, president of Lifetime Television, writes out her goals for that year. She finds it helpful to consider both her personal and professional objectives because both are important, and she has a tendency to shortchange the personal. Then she leaves the summary in a drawer, where she periodically glances at it before completing a final review of her accomplishments at the end of the year.

Betsy Holden, executive vice president of Kraft, participated in a work/life seminar at Kraft that she found particularly enlightening. It guided participants to examine seven areas of life—physical health, spiritual health, social relationships (friends, and so on), family (including spouse, although this could be a separate area), community, personal, and professional. The seminar objective was to help participants set goals and priorities in the different areas in order to find the solution that worked best for each person, while recognizing that it is not possible to optimize all seven simultaneously. At different phases of your life, different areas play a more important role. For example, earlier in your adult life, you may focus on career, spouse, and friends, and then focus less on some of these if you have children. For each area, seminar participants completed a self-assessment and articulated goals. Then they crafted personal mission statements that incorporated their ideas. Considering these seven areas can help you to be more thoughtful and thorough in setting your own goals. The key, however, is to be honest with yourself about what you want and how you plan to get there.

You may want to collaborate on the personal and professional planning exercise with a spouse or partner. Holden, a mother of two, sits down with her husband once per year to address their family plan, which includes professional objectives for both Betsy and her husband, a biotech executive. Employing a technique from work, Betsy seeks "360 degree" feedback by soliciting input from her kids regarding their perception of the family balance. Holden reviews their rolling five-year plan annually and her mission statement every few months to see how she's doing. Her personal experience leads her to advise, "Write a personal mission statement yourself, and then bring in your spouse. It helps to have what's important to you on paper because life is hectic and you frequently have to make quick trade-offs."

Holden's personal mission statement, which she terms a guiding force, helps her to prioritize what's important and what trade-offs to make. It also is helpful to her in evaluating extracurricular activities. In fact, Holden recently organized a session at her church retreat that used Stephen Covey's book about families, *The 7 Habits of Highly Effective Families*, to guide the group in creating personal and family mission statements. Holden and the others then spent an afternoon with their families thinking about what they hoped to accomplish.

While having a written plan is an effective tool for your own personal and professional development, it certainly is not a requirement for success. Alison Ressler, partner at Sullivan & Cromwell and mother of four, has no written plans. She doesn't believe in it, and thinks, instead, that you just need to know what's important to you. Ressler is not alone. Fewer than half of the women I interviewed actually write out their objectives. But don't discount the significant percentage of leaders who do commit their thoughts to paper. Particularly if you are not crystal clear regarding your own objectives and values, the exercise of writing a personal mission statement is especially enlightening. Try it and see if it helps you to organize your life more effectively and efficiently.

Remain Flexible and, Above All, Opportunistic

WHETHER YOU WRITE your goals or not, and whether they include your personal objectives and commitments or not, an absolutely critical component to success is to balance your focus with flexibility. First, recognize that there are many paths to a particular point. And second, accept that the point toward which you are aimed may not always be the optimal target. To coin some sports terms: Stay on your toes. Be nimble. Seize opportunities. Stay flexible.

Being flexible at work benefits you, your colleagues, and your company on many levels. At the most basic, flexibility in your work style enables you to interact successfully with a broad array of people. Cynthia Round learned flexibility in Italy, where her job was to introduce the product Pampers to the Italian market. Upon her arrival, she was a lone female executive who had barely traveled beyond her home state, let alone out of the country. She did not speak the language. And she quickly realized that she needed to adopt a whole new approach to getting business done. The old rules and work style she learned on the job back in the United States no longer applied. Further, in Italy, Round could not fall back on her own ability to get the job done. She had to trust and rely on others and bring out the best in them. The two years Round spent in Italy were a challenge, but she learned lessons that she's carried with her through the rest of her career.

> CYNTHIA Round did not plan her career, but she has been smart and flexible enough to recognize opportunity and seize it. She counsels, "Find the best job you can and then be ready and aware enough that you can jump on opportunities. I never said, 'I want to do X, so these are the twelve correct steps to get there.' Instead, I decided when it was time to move on and what was the best option."

Flexibility regarding your schedule or location of employment also benefits you and your company, although it can be a challenge for those who depend on you, such as a spouse or children. Therefore, take advantage of the flexibility that you often have earlier in your career, before there are as many competing demands on your time, to build experience and expertise. Geographic moves, while intimidating to

Cynthia Round

CYNTHIA GREW UP in a small town in Oklahoma and was the oldest of four children in her family. As both her parents worked, she learned to be responsible for her siblings, baby-sitting her two sisters and brother all summer from the time she was twelve. She also learned that a job equals financial freedom and developed the sense that she didn't want anyone to dictate how she should feel because they were paying the bills. Cynthia's parents provided strong values and imbued in her a strong sense of self. Additionally, they consistently rewarded accomplishment at home and at school. They conveyed to her that she could do and be whatever she wanted—although they never envisioned large horizons.

At thirteen, Cynthia, for a school project, decided she wanted to be an international flight attendant so she could see the world. Over time, the "world" objective stayed, while the career goal changed. When Cynthia left for Okalahoma State University, forty miles away, she became the first in her family to attend a college. There, Cynthia quickly learned to excel, joined many organizations, and set her sights on a 4.0 grade point average. When Cynthia flew to Cincinnati for an interview with Procter & Gamble, it was her first flight. When she accepted a job in 1975 selling soap, she was the only woman in the Oklahoma district. However, after six weeks, she felt she'd made a mistake and resigned to take a public relations job with Phillip's

Petroleum. But her boss didn't want her to go; he convinced her to attend a training program in Cincinnati and make a six-month commitment to sales, after which time they would find an advertising or public relations opportunity at Procter & Gamble if she still wanted it. Thus, Cynthia became one of 20 women in the 350-person marketing department, and had no idea that she had competed for a spot with Harvard graduates. At twenty-four, she was the youngest person to be made a brand manager. Acting on her wanderlust, Cynthia volunteered to go abroad, even though the businesses were smaller, and it was not considered a great career move then. She went to Italy to market Pampers, and considers her two years there the most challenging yet most rewarding time in her career.

Cynthia returned to the United States for personal reasons, but, having worked in Rome, felt a desire for the big city life that New York offered. Therefore, in 1982, Cynthia joined four ex-Procter & Gamble colleagues in a small consulting firm, American Consulting Corporation. A year later, she jumped to the agency side, joining Ogilvy & Mather, so that she could develop expertise as a positioning and brand-building specialist. From 1983 through 1998, Cynthia rose through the ranks and became a senior partner/executive group director and operating board member. In 1998, she went out on her own as a brand consultant.

Cynthia serves as chairman of the board for SoHo Repertory Theatre and as a member of the Oklahoma State University Board of Governors. She and her husband have one daughter.

some, provide terrific learning opportunities. Jackie Woods, president of Ameritech Ohio, has moved six times for either her job or her husband's, and each time she has gained valuable experience. Woods is one of those people who knew from the start what she wanted—but fortunately, she was not committed to one way to get there. She was flexible enough to recognize that there is more than one road to the top.

Shortly after Woods was hired by Ameritech Ohio in 1970, she realized that one day she would like to be president. In 1984, having climbed the ranks on the marketing side, Woods intended to leave the company because she perceived an engineering degree to be a prerequisite to the presidency. Instead, she was moved within the company to help form Ohio Bell Communications, the equipment marketing subsidiary. In 1989, Woods was transferred to Chicago to be vice president of finance and administration for Ameritech Services, moving from a job that required a marketing and sales orientation to one that demanded finance.

Flexibility in your work style enables you to interact successfully with a broad array of people.

The only way to survive was to be comfortable with numbers and financial analyses, so Woods took a course at night—in which she was the only woman—to build those skills. At the time she didn't see where it would lead her. Ultimately, it led her to the top, for in today's deregulated environment, an engineering degree is not essential to run Ameritech Ohio. Marketing and finance skills are.

A flexible approach, such as that employed by Jackie Woods, helps you to identify and take advantage of opportunities—even if these opportunities were not originally anticipated. Unfortunately, for some people, if reality doesn't match their theories, they don't recognize opportunity, or else they feel like a failure if they deviate from their plans. Avoid that trap by defining goals and paths broadly enough to give yourself some room.

Openness to new learning opportunities is critical to success. It requires not only flexibility but also a certain amount of confidence and risk-taking—confidence in yourself that you can adapt to and thrive in new situations, and the ability to risk moving from areas you know well into the unknown territory of a new opportunity. Janet Robinson's flexibility and openness to new opportunities resulted in a career path that included teaching and advertising sales before she was tapped to run the *New York Times*. During her tenure at the *New York Times,* Robinson not only switched cities once, but also became familiar with many of the newspaper's departments—including marketing, circulation, and strategic planning—while working in advertising and before taking on the role of president. For Robinson, her broad experience was like an on-the-job business school. It also illustrates the importance of getting your foot in the door to prove what you can do. One might not have expected Robinson, a former schoolteacher who was hired into the advertising department, to end up running the newspaper. She notes, "If you are talented, that talent should show, no matter what position you hold."

Flexibility begins with attitude. You can't wed yourself so rigidly to one objective or vision of yourself that you fail to recognize opportunity. If Janet Robinson had seen herself only as a teacher or advertising executive, she would have

Jacqueline Woods

JACKIE GREW UP in Ohio as an only child. Her father was a police lieutenant and her mom was a nurse and a volunteer for the Red Cross. While her father was serious and ruled the family, all was open to discussion (though not question).

Jackie planned to be a teacher and earned her teaching degree from Muskingum College in Ohio. However, when she met the man who eventually became her husband, she decided to take a job near him in Cleveland. Her first job was as an instructor and business office supervisor for Ohio Bell in 1970. She later held several positions in the customer service, public relations, public affairs, and marketing departments. During her career, she and her husband relocated a number of times to accommodate each other's work. In 1984 Jackie helped form Ohio Bell Communications, the company's equipment marketing subsidiary, and she later was named its president. In 1989, Jackie, with little background in finance, moved to Chicago to become vice president of finance and administration for Ameritech Services. She was named president and CEO of Ohio Bell in 1993, in time to oversee its transformation from Ohio Bell to Ameritech Ohio.

Jackie is active on numerous corporate, cultural, educational, and civic boards and has received many awards. She lives in Ohio with her husband and two daughters.

forgone opportunities to learn so many other areas of business—areas that provided her with the requisite skill set to lead a company.

The key to success is to recognize opportunity, even when it isn't on your defined path. Paula Sneed, one of the more extensive planners I interviewed, deviated from her plan a number of times with excellent results. First, as a director of a group of smaller brands at General Foods, Sneed anticipated that her next job would be director of a larger group of brands. Instead, she was offered vice president of consumer affairs, a staff position. Many of her colleagues counseled her that a staff job (versus a line job that has profit/ loss business responsibility) would take her off the path. "What," they said, "will your next job be?" Rather than be deterred, Sneed recognized the opportunity to learn a different side of the

MARY Ludgin's career path took so many turns she never could have predicted or aspired to her current job, as CEO of Heitman Capital Management. Ludgin began as a Ph.D. candidate and thought she might teach. Instead, she wound up in the planning department for the city of Chicago. From there she went to JMB Realty Corporation, and then followed her mentor to Heitman. She notes, "For a long time, even in real estate, my job as a researcher was not core and was a tiny piece of the whole, so I would never have set as a goal to become COO or CEO. However, each opportunity has come from the previous place. If you focus, work hard, and are flexible, something will come."

business, work for a terrific manager, and oversee an area not usually run by a business person. And, true to the promise of her superiors, her next position, senior vice president of General Foods USA and president of the foodservice division, returned Sneed, at a higher level, to line (profit/loss business) responsibility.

Flexibility begins with attitude. You can't wed yourself so rigidly to one objective or vision of yourself that you fail to recognize opportunity.

Why is line responsibility critical? This discussion is a sidepoint to the chapter, but it is, nonetheless, important. Line responsibility places you where corporate America focuses—on core business and profitability. Thus, if you work for a consumer products company, moving up the ladder in human resources, for example, will not prepare you to run the company. Instead, you need experience running the soap, or toaster, or cheese business. Historically, women have gravitated to staff positions, leaving them ill-prepared to ascend to the highest rungs of the ladder. A recent study by Catalyst found that the small percentage of women holding line officer jobs—6.8 percent—is limiting their advancement to the highest echelons of power. Catalyst president Sheila Wellington notes that, "until more women move into line positions, you won't find women in many corner offices."

Take Stock of Your Progress

HOWEVER YOU USE goals to help you achieve, it is important to periodically step back from the day-to-day grind to examine how you're doing. It is easy to get lost in the proverbial trees and miss the forest. It is also easy to take incremental step after incremental step to a place where you really don't want to be. Sometimes it takes the greatest courage to stop the merry-go-round and get off. At the very least, take a few moments between rides to reflect.

Each year Jane Thompson travels to St. Barts with her husband. And each year, "while we're there," Thompson notes, "I reflect upon personal and professional goals and write an annual letter to the kids which includes fun things we did that year and values. I take the old letters and goals with me to review." This routine enables Thompson to step back physically and emotionally, take stock, and plan for the future.

Robin Foote began taking stock at age 39, during a seminar in the Canadian Rockies that combined mountaineering with reflections on life. As she stepped back to reassess, she realized she had allowed work to dominate her life and that she'd made too many decisions by default—particularly around the balance between work and play. She says: "I recognized the need to redress this imbalance and decided to anchor it with an annual trip to the mountains. As well, I started spending more time with family and friends, which proved very nourishing. To my surprise and delight, I found I was even more effective at work!"

◗ POWER POINTER *Put the right support network in place to maximize your focus and flexibility. Support systems are important to everyone, whether single or married, parent or not. "Going it alone" does not make you a superhero; instead, it reduces your chance of success. Therefore, evaluate what support could help you, and strive to secure the appropriate resources.*

Betsy Holden has an extensive support system in place that allows her and her husband to excel at fast-paced jobs. Together, they raise two children. Her network includes her husband, her sister, friends, a nanny, the nanny's mom, and her friends at Kraft. Betsy is able to accomplish so much because she applies some of the same rigorous business principles she relies on at work in her home. For example, as you'll see in chapter nine, when Betsy moves forward with plan A, she always has contingency plans B, C, and D in place. Therefore at home, if her nanny is sick, Holden has a number of viable alternatives for making sure that her children are well cared for while she is engaged at work. As another friend of mine once said regarding childcare, "If you are down to one, you are down to none." Keep several options available to maintain a smoothly functioning work and family life.

Even without children, a support network is vital to long-term success. The demands are great at any level in any industry, and to focus on doing your best requires harmony in other parts of your life, whatever they may be. Veronica Biggins, a partner at the executive search firm Heidrick & Struggles, notes, "Every woman needs a wife." What she really is saying is that everyone needs someone who can back her or him and provide support—at home as well as on the job.

CHAPTER TWO SUMMARY AT-A-GLANCE

Use the checklist below to make sure you understand the points and steps discussed in chapter two.

Focus on doing the best you can do at your current job.

Focus on goals that can guide you.
- ☑ Using stretch goals that can serve as beacons.
- ☑ Using incremental goals.
- ☑ Employing a milestone approach, which utilizes immediate and stretch goals.

Tailor your own approach to goal-setting.
- ☑ Change your approach as necessary.
- ☑ Commit goals to paper, especially the first time.
- ☑ Include personal goals as well as professional goals.

Remain flexible and, above all, opportunistic.
- ☑ Be flexible with your work style, schedule, location, and path.
- ☑ Recognize opportunity.

Take stock periodically to see how you're doing.
- ☑ Step back from day-to-day responsibilities to reflect.
- ☑ Ensure that the path you are on is taking you where you want to go.

You Never Know Where the Next Idea Will Come From

 POWER POINTER *Seek feedback aggressively and don't personalize what you hear.*

B E A LIFE-LONG learner. Be curious; you never know where the next idea will come from. Be open to ideas from all sources," counsels Rose Marie Bravo, chief executive of Burberry.

You can and do learn all the time. Even when you're tuning out in front of the television, you are learning something about the world around you. Today's leaders understand the power of knowledge, and they put to good use the vast information they gather through everyday life.

There are three primary techniques that you can employ to make the most of every experience and be systematic in your approach to gaining knowledge. They include:

1. be a student of the world;
2. use education and on-the-job training to build your knowledge base; and
3. seek and use feedback constructively.

48

These strategies will help you not only to learn more and have more fun but also to recognize and better utilize the knowledge that is already yours.

Be a Student of the World

THE WORLD IS one big classroom. Whether you like to read books, magazines, or newspapers, explore cyberspace, chat with neighbors, see movies, wander through new neighborhoods, or travel the world (by foot, bicycle, car, train, or plane), your five senses are constantly receiving information. For example, if you work in the special events department at your company, you may get an idea for an employee event from *People* magazine as easily as from *Forbes*. And, who knows, that science fiction reading habit may help you when your advertising company lands a new high-tech client who wants a futuristic campaign. The trick is to

YOU need to be aware of your environment and not recede into your own world. It takes work to stay current. And it gets harder as you get older and your time is stretched thinner," notes Mary Baglivo, executive vice president of J. Walter Thompson and former CEO of the advertising agency Euro RSCG Tatham. Baglivo pushes herself to attend concerts and movies and explore different facets of her community and the world. You're probably already doing many of these activities yourself, but not necessarily recognizing that every experience adds to your knowledge base and ultimately can serve you well.

Carole Black

CAROLE GREW UP in Cincinnati with her mom, who divorced when Carole was six months old, her sister, and her grandparents, who were the most influential people in her life. Carole's grandfather was born in Armenia and self-educated, but he became so successful he was once named "businessman of the year" in Cincinnati. He told Carole, "This is a great country. You are smart, and there is nothing you can't do." While her grandfather instilled Carole with drive and confidence, her grandmother taught her the value of people and relationships through her example of generosity, caring, and doing for others.

Carole earned a BA in English literature from Ohio State University and began her career in brand management at Procter & Gamble. From 1983 to 1986, Black worked at DDB Needham in Chicago, where she rose from account supervisor to senior vice president. She then worked at Disney as vice president of worldwide marketing, home video, for two years, then became senior vice president of marketing, television, from 1988 to 1994. In 1994, she switched gears and was appointed president of NBC4 Los Angeles. There, she quickly took the television station from a weak number two in the market to a dominant number one position. Under her stewardship, the company and Carole won numerous awards. In 1999, Carole became president and CEO of Lifetime Television.

Carole is divorced and has one son.

recognize that you are learning all the time and, through practice, to become more comfortable with using all that data that you have advertantly or inadvertently stored.

It's hard to believe, but in 1986, Disney's focus for its film library was on the rental market. Previously, Disney had released just one film for sale—*Pinocchio*—and it sold just three hundred thousand copies. Carole Black believed that, marketed correctly, Disney could sell millions of vidoes on individual titles to consumers. When she interviewed for the job of vice president for worldwide marketing, home video, for Disney in 1986, her interviewer thought she was "over-the-top" with her projections, but he liked the spirit of her ideas.

How was Black able to see the tremendous value of the video sales market when it virtually did not exist at that time? She pulled together knowledge accumulated on many different fronts to craft her prescient vision. First, from her professional experience at Procter & Gamble, she had analyzed the female consumer. Second, as a representative of the female target market, she had her own experiences and judgments from which to draw. Third, as a parent, she recognized that kids love repetition. Fourth, from her work on the Sears account while she was at advertising agency DDB Needham, Black had insight into the "nesting" trend—the term coined by Faith Popcorn to describe America's growing interest in the comforts of the home. Black put together these disparate pieces of data and, using her intuition, laid out a strategy for Disney to sell videos to consumers. She was hired on the spot. Her knowledge and intuition helped her to see where the business could go, and it earned her the job. It also earned significant profits for her employer, for during Black's two years in the position, Disney sold ten million tapes. Without drawing on experiences accumulated through both her professional and personal lives, Black wouldn't have been able to pull it all together.

Stretching yourself beyond your usual horizons is important. It doesn't have to be expensive or uncomfortable. Just different. If you enjoy going to rock concerts, mix them up sometime with the local symphony—and vice versa. You will see different people and lifestyles, and that, likely, will impact your view of the world. If you find you go repeatedly to the same restaurants, pick one in a different neighborhood. Break your routine occasionally, and you'll be amazed at what you discover.

Ask Probing Questions

An attitude of curiosity and an inclination to question are characteristic of those people who are life-long learners. As your first-grade teacher probably told you, there are no dumb questions. Don't hesitate to question your personal and professional acquaintances about their lives and experience. The benefits will be at least three-fold: (1) the people you talk to will be flattered by your interest in them and their areas of expertise; (2) you'll show that you are thoughtful and interested; and (3) you'll learn a tremendous amount.

Stay Current in a Changing Environment

You're never too old to learn. An openness to new opportunities and to seizing chances to learn and build skills will serve anyone well in any endeavor. When Federated Department Stores sold Foley's to May Company, a much more centralized organization, Janet Gurwitch Bristow's mentor,

Foley's chairman Michael Steinberg, was fifty-seven years old. Gurwitch Bristow was not certain Steinberg would be able to adapt and do things a new way under the new owner. But he rose to the occasion, recognizing that there was a lot to learn. It was from Steinberg that Gurwitch Bristow learned the concept of being a perpetual "student of the business."

Today, you never really "know your business" because most businesses change rapidly. Those who are complacent get left behind. And that's an opportunity for you. Stay alert and on top of your game, and you'll be able to pass by those who stand still. If you're in an office support function, that could mean developing new computer skills to help get maximum benefit from the technology your company has invested in. For Janet Gurwitch Bristow, when she ran the cosmetics division for Neiman Marcus, it meant recognizing and anticipating the growing importance of niche cosmetics brands. Retailers like Neiman Marcus that saw the future before everyone else benefited most. Gurwitch Bristow not only positioned Neiman Marcus beautifully, she also recognized a key business opportunity for herself. Gurwitch Bristow is founder and CEO of Gurwitch Bristow Products, which produces Laura Mercier Cosmetics.

Break your routine occasionally, and you'll be amazed at what you discover.

LEARN FROM NEGATIVE SITUATIONS

There is no such thing as a situation from which you don't learn. And that includes "bad experiences." In fact, sometimes you can learn the most important lessons from mis-

Janet Gurwitch Bristow

JANET AND HER younger brother were born and raised in Hattiesburg, Mississippi. Her father owned a small group of shoestores, and while her mom stayed at home, everything she did, she did brilliantly. Janet's only professional woman role model in Hattiesburg was her pediatrician. However, Janet's parents believed in her and provided tremendous support throughout her academic and professional careers.

Janet earned her BS degree from the University of Alabama, where she received many honors. When she sent her resume to Foley's executive management program, she received a reply stating that the company didn't interview at her school. Therefore, she went to Houston, presented herself in person, and got the job.

During eighteen years with Foley's, a division of the May Company, Janet rose through the ranks from entry-level executive to senior vice president and general merchandise manager. Janet also served as executive vice president of women's merchandising at Neiman Marcus. In 1994, her area of responsibility contributed over $1.1 billion in revenues—80 percent of the store's business. In 1995, Janet resigned her job to found Gurwitch Bristow Products, the manufacturer and marketer of the fast-growing Laura Mercier line of cosmetics.

Janet and her husband reside in the Houston area.

takes, both yours and those of others. As my husband often says, If you're given lemons, make lemonade. Turn your failures into successes by extracting the appropriate lessons. Ask yourself what you or someone else could have done differently to achieve a more positive outcome. Which signals could you have recognized earlier? What changes could you have made to your plan and execution to mitigate your loss or increase your success? Reviewing projects and assignments—looking at both positives and negatives—can help you to avoid pitfalls and operate more effectively and efficiently in the future.

LEARN FROM THE PEOPLE YOU MEET

You never know where the next idea will come from, so be open to learning from anyone. You can get good business ideas from people with no business background, just as you can garner insights and ideas from those at all levels and in all roles within your company or industry. Suzanne Nora Johnson tries to emulate traits that she admires in others. Suzanne has garnered lessons regarding how to deal with adversity and how to be generous with others from a broad group of people, some who she knows and some who she's read about. They include Jackie Ferrari and Julie Montgomery, her administrative assistants at Goldman Sachs, and Mother Teresa and Oprah Winfrey. The bottom line is: Create value out of every encounter.

You can learn from positive as well as negative role models—whether a difficult boss or a challenging employee. Barbara Allen, the chief operating officer of Paladin Resources and former executive vice president at The Quaker Oats Company, was warned a couple of times as she climbed the ladder at Quaker that she had a "bad" boss. Rather than be deterred by her boss's reputation, Allen took it as a challenge to figure out what was important to that person and to deliver her own side of the equation. By not "pre-judging," but instead trying to understand her colleague's work style, Allen found that she still could achieve for herself and her company in a tough situation. However, if you believe there is nothing someone can teach you, then you won't learn.

Once, Allen's "bad boss" was so committed to his plan of action that he ignored contradictory data that Allen presented. Did Allen get dejected and decide extensive research wasn't worth the effort? No. Instead, she worked harder to (a) verify her data and (b) develop measurable milestones so that her team would know quickly whether they were following the correct or incorrect path. And, a week later, when the president asked Allen what she thought, she was able to succinctly explain her different point of view. Once the president reviewed the new data, he canceled the project.

Even a bad boss has good qualities, and you can learn

> ROLE models provide excellent learning opportunities. Lindy Hirschsohn, a partner at The Boston Consulting Group (BCG), recognized early on that she didn't have all the answers and skills and would have to engage in a BCG apprenticeship. Like Suzanne Nora Johnson, she learned from others by emulating the attributes she admired, and then packaging those qualities with her own unique touch. That's a strategy that can work for anyone.

from both the positives and negatives. From her boss's negative traits, Allen learned that (1) decision makers aren't always rational and data isn't the only input, and (2) she must be sensitive to overly committing herself to a particular plan, lest she be blind to data.

And, from his positive side, Allen learned to prepare amply for meetings with senior executives. At first, Allen thought her boss overprepared to a point that was ridiculous. He reviewed his presentation repeatedly, ultimately cutting it to its essence.

Even a bad boss has good qualities, and you can learn from both the positives and negatives.

Eventually, Allen realized that she had been underpreparing and it was hampering her development. Now she reviews her presentations several times and is grateful to her "bad boss" for this effective habit.

Allen's daughter once had a coach who overreacted and did not treat the players with respect. When her daughter complained, Allen asked her, "What did you learn from it? If you don't like it, then make sure you don't do it down the line." At the very least, when you find yourself in an unpalatable spot, seek the useful lesson, even if it's an example of how not to do something.

BE SYSTEMATIC ABOUT LEARNING

In addition to the informal learning that takes place daily, you can be systematic in your approach to building your knowledge base. Scanning magazines and books—or at least their reviews—helps to keep you current. So does attending the right conferences and being out and about talking to others in similar positions or industries. Indra Nooyi cites

Barbara Allen

BARB GREW UP on the south side of Chicago, one of three girls in her family. Her mom was widowed young, and though she hadn't gone to college herself, she taught her children the importance of education, as well as self-sufficiency, persistence, and the value of family. Today, Barb and her sisters are each working moms in the business world.

Barb was not aware growing up that there were "jobs for males and for females." Barb considers that ignorance bliss, as she didn't know that there were things that women were "not supposed to do."

Barb graduated from the University of Illinois with a degree in psychology, and she earned her MBA from the University of Chicago. She began her career at the Quaker Oats Company in 1975 as a marketing assistant and rose through the ranks to executive vice president of international foods. During her twenty-four-year career with Quaker, she became the first woman to run an operating division and the first woman at Quaker to have a child with the intention of returning to work.

Barb joined Corporate Express as president of Corporate Supplier Solutions in 1998. At the start of the new millenium, she left the world of billion-dollar companies to become CEO of an Internet start-up, Paladin Resources. Barb serves on the board of directors of the Maytag Corporation and Charthouse Restaurants.

Barb lives in Colorado with her husband and two children.

knowledge as a key to her success. She knows her material, and it's not an accident. She works at it. Nooyi stays on the cutting edge of strategy—a key job responsibility as senior vice president and CFO at PepsiCo—by speed-reading voraciously all the new books on related topics. She also gives speeches. On the surface, it would appear that speech-making helps her to dispense information. However, it also helps her to gather it, since giving speeches ensures that she's out in the field and in the information flow. Nooyi listens closely for new ideas and considers intently how they can help PepsiCo. While Nooyi prefers to listen, she makes herself heard when necessary, and she constantly adds to her bag of tricks.

I try to scan the four newspapers that arrive at our house daily and the five business magazines that come to our door-step weekly as well as numerous other catalogs and publications. Of course, it's impossible to read every word or article. My grandmother, a "value maximizer," canceled her daily newspaper delivery and just subscribed on Sundays, because by reading the paper literally cover-to-cover she was busy all week. Wait until you're ninety for that, since you learn more by scanning more broadly.

Use Education and On-the-Job Training to Build Your Knowledge Base

THERE IS NO question, a solid education can help prepare you for a successful career. Of the forty-five women I interviewed for this book, 60 percent have graduate degrees. By far, the most common graduate degree for this group of business phenomenons is an MBA. If you aspire to climb the ladder at a large company or to raise money for an entrepreneurial venture, having the right pedigree can add skills and credibility, thereby helping you to succeed.

CONSIDER A GRADUATE DEGREE

There are many routes you can choose to secure a graduate degree. Pursuing it full-time is the least-stressful, most-costly alternative. An advantage of this approach is that you'll have the greatest opportunity to throw yourself into the school's activities and really get to know people. Unquestionably, one of the most valuable byproducts from an MBA is the network of contacts you develop. The advantage of pursuing an MBA at night or through some other part-time program is that you'll be able to continue on your professional track and continue to earn your salary. Additionally, large companies will frequently pay for the coursework while you are an employee, and you'll likely meet others in similar situations who are juggling interesting careers and classes. Many top MBA programs provide a selection of part-time opportunities ranging from evening classes to weekend and summer programs. These options are designed for business people who would like the education without having to give up their jobs and income.

Distance learning opportunities—degree and non-degree—are proliferating with the Internet. While there were 710,000 U.S. students in distance-learning programs in 1998 (4.8 percent of the 14.6 million students overall), International Data Corporation forecasts that, by 2002, the number will grow to 2.23 million (or 14.8 percent of the estimated 15.1 million students overall). Schools as prestigious as Wharton and Stanford offer classes and degree programs that enable you to download lectures, submit papers, join in student discussions, and get your grades over the Internet. These programs essentially bring the classroom to you, on your terms, in your time frame.

A graduate degree can be particularly helpful if you are interested in changing industries. First, you'll benefit from classes in your intended field. Second, if you are a full-time student, a summer job at a company at which you might want to work will prepare you with relevant job experience. Third, you'll have access to the broad spectrum of recruiters who seek candidates from your school.

The women leaders I interviewed valued their degrees and generally recommended an MBA for others interested in business success. Mary Ludgin, who has two masters degrees, neither of which is an MBA, suggests that if you don't already have a graduate degree, you add that into your five-year plan. And Sheri Wilson-Gray, who attended the Krannert School of Management at Purdue University, advises that if you go for an MBA, go to a blue-chip school. The validation of a well-respected program makes people take you more seriously. I think that advice is correct. You should always go to the best program that you can, given your credentials and your wallet.

Is a graduate degree imperative for success? Absolutely not. If you are progressing nicely at a company that you enjoy, an MBA may be less beneficial. However, down the line, should you decide to change jobs or industries, you may wish you had the degree. Therefore, it is worthwhile to consider pursuing your graduate work part-time. Another option, however, is executive education programs. These courses, such as the top-rated ones at Kellogg and Harvard, are designed as quick knowledge enhancers for seasoned executives. They typically range in length from two to six days and provide top professors, stimulating dialogue with accomplished participants, state-of-the-art thinking, and the chance to step back from your day-to-day grind and expand your network with new colleagues. Executive education is not only a time-efficient option but a more affordable one, as your employer often will pick up the tab.

GET TRAINED ON THE JOB

For anyone coming out of school, particularly if you don't have a graduate degree, choosing a company with a strong training program can pay real dividends. A company with a commitment to train you will invest in your development and can usually afford to deploy dollars that help you to learn on the job. After Sheri Wilson-Gray completed her MBA, she worked at Procter & Gamble—known as a terrific training ground for aspiring marketing executives. There, Wilson-Gray gained exposure to television and radio advertising—something she wouldn't have had the resources for at a smaller company. She also had the luxury of test-markets and could learn all about that aspect of product research on Procter & Gamble's dime. When Wilson-Gray moved on to a company that couldn't afford that training, her experience was especially valuable. For Wilson-Gray, Procter & Gamble provided an opportunity to invest in herself with someone else's resources.

If you make a commitment to education, whether at school or on the job, you'll build a strong foundation for yourself—and common sense dictates that it's hard to reach great heights without a strong foundation. Therefore, it is not a coincidence that a significant number of women I interviewed began their careers in corporate training programs or worked for large firms that invested significant resources in their growth. Procter & Gamble provided the professional start for Cynthia Round, who became a senior partner at Ogilvy & Mather advertising agency before hanging out her own shingle as a brand consultant; Jane Thompson, who rose to partner at McKinsey & Company before leaving to run a succession of businesses at Sears and elsewhere; and Sheri Wilson-Gray, who took on a number of consumer products marketing positions before settling in at Saks Fifth Avenue, where she is executive vice president. In the retail field, Bloomingdale's training program spawned, among others, Robin Burns, president and CEO of Victoria's Secret Beauty and Intimate Beauty Corporation; Sue Kronick, chairman and CEO of Burdine's department stores; and Andrea Jung, CEO of Avon.

If you make a commitment to education, whether at school or on the job, you'll build a strong foundation for yourself—and common sense dictates that it's hard to reach great heights without a strong foundation.

I have found that management consulting provides an excellent training ground for any business endeavor. The problem-solving approach that you learn is rigorous and flexible. And the firm invests heavily in tenure-specific and industry-specific training throughout your career. Not surprisingly, alumni from leading management consulting companies are running many of the country's top businesses. The CEOs of IBM, Morgan Stanley Dean Witter, Ameri-

Jane J. Thompson

JANE, BORN IN 1951, was the oldest of three girls in her family. Her mom was a nurse and her dad was a union pipe fitter. In high school, Jane became the star forward of the St. Albans Highlawn Baptist basketball team, which her mother coached, and this experience inspired her competitive drive, team orientation, and love of winning. Jane was the first in her family to earn a college degree—a bachelor's degree in business from the University of Cincinnati. Jane's practical side led her to pursue business as an undergraduate so she could more easily find a job when she was done. Upon graduation, Jane worked at Procter & Gamble, where she was promoted to brand manager within four years. While there, she helped to hire Cynthia Round, also interviewed for this book. By the time Jane left to attend Harvard Business School, she was the second-most senior woman in marketing.

Following her graduation from Harvard Business School, Jane began a ten-year career at McKinsey, in which she rose to partner and coleader of the consumer goods and retailing practice. In 1988, she joined Sears, Roebuck, and Company as vice president of planning with the objective to run a business. She spent the first four years in planning, including working closely with CEO Arthur Martinez to design the strategy credited with turning Sears around. From 1993 to 1995, Jane served as executive vice president and general manager of the Sears Credit Group and chairman of the board and CEO of Sears National Bank. In 1996, Jane was named president of Sears Home Services, and in 1998 became president of the newly formed Sears Direct. In 1999, she shifted gears and joined the entrepreneurial InLight Incorporated, an online e-health company, as president and chief operating officer.

Jane is on the board of directors of ConAgra, Inc., a Fortune 50 company in Nebraska. In the Chicago area, Jane serves as chairman of the board of the Boys and Girls Club of Chicago and the Chicago Network, and as a member of the board of Children's Memorial Hospital. She is a member of the Commercial Club of Chicago, the Economic Club of Chicago, the Harvard Business School Club of Chicago, Committee of 200, Chicago Committee of the Council on Foreign Relations, and the Executives Club of Chicago. Jane has been recognized for her leadership by numerous publications.

Jane resides with her husband, a corporate executive, and their two children, outside of Chicago. Despite a heavy travel schedule, she has served as assistant coach for her daughter's basketball team and still loves competitive sports.

can Express, Delta Airlines, and Polaroid, among others, all hail from McKinsey. So does Sharon Patrick, president of Martha Stewart Living Omnimedia.

General Electric is renowned for its deep management ranks—layers and layers of men and women whose talents have been cultivated internally. The company, which generally does not hire people with fancy business degrees, also develops managers through tons of formal education and training, frequent performance reviews, and exposure to disparate businesses, which provides executives with more ideas and confidence than most people acquire on their own. As *Fortune* magazine noted in its August, 2, 1999 article entitled, "CEO Super Bowl," General Electric has been as successful a breeding ground for senior executives as McKinsey, which routinely recruits from top schools. General Electric's "alumni" now run Allied Signal, SPX, USF&G, Stanley Works, Owens Corning, and Merix Corporation, among others. As you can see, the particular type of training you choose does not matter. The key is to get trained.

Gaining experience in many different parts of a company is an important benefit of a strong training program. For example, if you aspire to run a bank one day, look for a job at a place like Bank One, where the formal training program includes rotations to expose young executives to disparate areas of the bank. Many large companies routinely move promising managers around to different departments. If your company does not take that approach or you are not on that track, speak up. Let someone more senior know that you'd value the broad experience and that the company's investment in you will pay off through your increased perspective and understanding of the entire company. Colleen Barrett notes, "I really encourage people at almost every level, entry through officer, to do a lot of department-hopping to get a broad exposure." Barrett has found that this breadth of experience helps Southwest Airlines and the individual employee find the right job fit, that it creates "smarter" employees with more business education, and that it enables people to move up the ladder to senior management.

YOU NEVER KNOW WHAT EXPERIENCE WILL BE VALUABLE LATER

You never know precisely how and when something you learned along the way will be valuable, but every job, even the most menial, adds to your knowledge. Robin Burns, who went into Bloomingdale's training program after college, remembers standing in a warehouse supervising inventory and thinking, "I went to college for this?" But years later, she reflected back on that experience during a lengthy meeting regarding inventory issues as president of Estee Lauder USA and Canada. Burns took away two lessons from that sequence: (1) there is no such thing as an experience where you don't learn, and (2) you may have to do things that you don't like but which are necessary as you climb the ladder.

> *You never know precisely how and when something you learned along the way will be valuable, but every job, even the most menial, adds to your knowledge.*

Seek and Use Feedback Constructively

SEEKING FEEDBACK FROM those around you is one of the best ways to gauge how you're doing and learn how you might improve your performance. While most companies have periodic reviews, you'll be well served by taking the initiative yourself to survey colleagues and those around you. Knowledge is power, particularly about yourself. And it's hard to see yourself as others see you.

ASK EARLY

You can't address issues if you don't know about them. Don't wait until the end of a project to seek feedback. There is nothing more frustrating than finding out at the conclusion of an endeavor that you should have done something differently, especially were it in your power to effect the change. Barb Allen goes so far as to recommend, "If people are not willing to share feedback with you, then find a place that is, because that is where you need to be to succeed."

Asking for feedback can feel uncomfortable because what you hear most often is what you are not doing well. However, it's easier to address issues early and head on. As part of Quaker's 360-degree reviews (in which you receive feedback from those all around you—above, at, and below your level), Barb Allen was told that her desk made her look like a leader out of control. Her first reaction was that if people wanted to worry about the appearance of her desk, they could take a hike. But then she realized that perception is important in leadership. The comment jolted her into looking around at the leaders in her company, and she saw more orderly offices. Now, Allen works hard to keep an organized look. Allen notes, "You need to get beyond, 'it's trivial,' and figure out why you got the feedback."

Be strategic about when you ask for or dispense feedback. I learned the hard way about the importance of timing, when my boss made a few "suggestions" while I was on maternity leave. I had weeks to stew over the comments before returning to work, where I could actually address the issue. From that time, I vowed, as a manager, never to dispense even constructive criticism when someone couldn't address it immediately. That means waiting until Monday morning rather than having a "parting conversation" Friday afternoon. It also means waiting until someone who is traveling returns to the office. Giving people the immediate opportunity following feedback to discuss a thought or address an issue is beneficial to everyone involved.

Lindy Hirschsohn credits early feedback with saving her career. At the time, she was a case leader on the verge of becoming a manager at The Boston Consulting Group (BCG) and had just been told by one of her team members, "We like you, but you're tough to work for. You and the vice president have ambitious goals, and you probably don't even realize that we are worn out. You assume we can all work at your pace and still sleep and eat."

Hirschsohn believes that this early feedback set her on the right course at The Boston Consulting Group. She always had intended to be a good manager—primarily, out of concern for her colleagues and, secondarily, because her own success depended on it. BCG has a market-driven system for staffing, so strong managers attract the strongest teams, while weak managers are weeded out.

Following this revealing feedback, Hirschsohn experienced a succession of emotions. First, she was surprised. She considered herself to work at an "average" pace within the talent pool at BCG, so it hadn't dawned on her that others would be challenged to keep up with her. Second, she felt

Lindy Hirschsohn

L INDY, WHO NOTES that she is "not smart enough to be the youngest," is the middle child in her family and was raised in South Africa. During her childhood, sports were important. Lindy did not have a killer instinct or care if she won or lost, but she loved being part of a team, exerting herself physically and having fun. She played team tennis and squash, and developed leadership skills as captain of a netball (like basketball) team.

Lindy's family stressed education and doing well in school, but they also encouraged an active interest in all aspects of life. Intellectual dinner conversations were common, and the range of topics included art, music, business, and politics. This broad exposure ignited her curiosity and gave her confidence to excel.

Lindy completed her undergraduate work at Cape Town University in South Africa and then worked at Research Surveys. She earned a masters in management from Kellogg Graduate School of Management at Northwestern University in 1987 and went on to work at The Boston Consulting Group (BCG), where she rose to partner.

Lindy and her husband have two young children. She is currently on leave-of-absence to focus on raising their children.

guilty and sorry that her team was unhappy with the experience she was providing.

Rather than becoming defensive, Hirschsohn reviewed her team's experiences and recognized that she needed to strengthen her prioritization skills. She had grown up thinking the more extensively one worked, the better, but she now realized that, as she put it, "you can only dig a few deep wells and need to keep the rest more shallow. The challenge, therefore, is to figure out which wells to dig deep." She explains, "I now subscribe to the philosophy that you focus on three major issues and keep the others on the back burner. But you only go to the back burner when there is nothing else that needs to be done."

Giving people the immediate opportunity following feedback to discuss a thought or address an issue is beneficial to everyone involved.

Armed with her new understanding, Hirschsohn consciously worked both to build her capability and to be more sensitive to her team's needs, and she improved markedly as a manager. She watched closely those with the skills she aspired to—the "brilliant triagers"—who served their clients well without driving their teams to exhaustion. And she continued to seek feedback from the people she worked with. While Hirschsohn was promoted to manager six months later, she honed her ability to focus and prioritize over the next one or two years and still works at it. With improved judgment over time, Hirschsohn became a partner at BCG and a popular team leader.

IDENTIFY STRENGTHS

Knowing what you do well can be as important as learning what needs to be fixed. While most people tend to think of feedback as focusing on weaknesses, use it also to identify and hone your strengths. Your strengths provide you with your advantage and your skill set, and they shouldn't be neglected as you work to alleviate weaknesses.

Focusing on strengths fosters business as well as individual development. One of Robin Burns's wonderful business "ahas" was that people in business tend to focus on what's not working and how to fix it more than they focus on something that's working and how to improve it. For example, Estee Lauder's business is approximately split between make-up, skin care, and fragrance. But there are markets where the fragrance business lags. Invariably, in those markets, the manager tries to build fragrance rather than capitalizing on the strengths of make-up and skin care. However, if the particular market in question is 80 percent Asian, and Asian women tend not to wear perfume, then there are cultural reasons for the disparity. In that instance, the manager is better off simply maintaining fragrance and focusing on building skin care. When she was president of Estee Lauder USA and Canada, Burns achieved strong results by focusing her team on individual and corporate strengths. You, too, will achieve superior results by focusing on building strengths.

TAKE ACTION TO HONE STRENGTHS AND CORRECT WEAKNESSES

To focus on strengths does not mean to ignore or give up on areas of perceived weakness. It is possible to turn a glaring weakness into a stand-out strength. It is also possible to improve upon your core competencies. Elynor Williams was told in a performance review at a previous company that her communication skills were weak. Williams was incredulous. She not only had a masters in communication from Cornell, but she believed communications to be one of her strengths. Based on her education, Williams might have discounted this surprising piece of feedback rather than confront it.

In order to prove the review was incorrect, Williams set a two-pronged skill development path for herself. To improve her writing, Williams began working with the editor of the company paper, who sent her on assignment. To improve her public speaking, Williams sought speaking engagements. I can personally attest to Williams's strength as a communicator. I first met Elynor Williams when she presented eloquently to the Leadership Illinois group, of which I was a part. She galvanized the audience with her clear and enthusiastic presentation. Thus, while William's communication skills were, indeed, strong, her proactive reaction to the criticism she received enabled her to strengthen them further and become stronger.

Williams's recognition of the importance of life-long learning and growth is reflected in her attitude and actions—as well as in "The Rules for Being Human," from the book *If Life Is a Game, These Are the Rules,* by Chérie Carter-Scott, PhD, that she gave me when I interviewed her for this book. It is a poignant statement regarding the "full-time informal school called Life." As Williams shared it with me, I now share it with you:

Elynor Williams

E LYNOR GREW UP in the South with her parents and older sister, Gwendolyn. Elynor learned from her father, an educator who founded a college, that she could do anything. She and her sister were raised to believe that they were special. Their parents expected them to get an education, do well, and give back to society—"to be and to help others be."

Elynor trained as a teacher and earned a bachelor's degree from Spelman College. Early in her career, the schools went on strike, and through a job fair, she secured a job with General Foods. When her mentor at General Foods suggested she go for a master's at Cornell, she did on scholarship. Following graduation, Williams worked at AT&T before transitioning to the Hanes group at Sara Lee. In 1983, Elynor became director of Corporate Affairs, and in 1990, vice president of corporate responsibility at Sara Lee.

In 2000, she left Sara Lee to become president and managing director of Chestnut Pearson & Associates, an international management consulting company.

Elynor is a founding board member of the Executive Leadership Council, Spelman College Corporate Women's Roundtable, and Leadership Illinois. She is a board member of the National Black Arts Festival, the American Cancer Society Foundation, and the Chicago Sinfonietta. She has been profiled in numerous publications and received many awards for professional achievements. She is single and resides in the Chicago area.

The Ten Rules for Being Human

- **Rule #1. You Will Receive a Body.** You may love it or hate it, but it will be yours for the duration of your life on Earth.
- **Rule #2. You Will Be Presented with Lessons.** You are enrolled in a full-time informal school called "life." Each day in this school you will have the opportunity to learn lessons. You may like the lessons or hate them, but you have designed them as part of your curriculum.
- **Rule #3. There Are No Mistakes, Only Lessons.** Growth is a process of trials, errors, and occasional victories. The <u>failed</u> experiments are as much a part of the process as the experiments that work.
- **Rule #4. Lessons Are Repeated Until Learned.** Lessons will be repeated to you in various forms until you have learned them. When you have learned them, you can then go on to the next lesson.
- **Rule #5. Learning Does Not End.** There is no part of life that does not contain lessons. If you are alive, there are lessons to be learned.
- **Rule #6. <u>There</u> is No Better Than Here.** When your "there" has become a "here," you will simply obtain another "there" that will look better to you than your present "here."
- **Rule #7. Others Are Only Mirrors of You.** You cannot love or hate something about another person unless it reflects something you love or hate about yourself.
- **Rule #8. What You Make of Your Life is Up to You.** You have all the tools and resources you need. What you do with them is up to you.
- **Rule #9. All Your Answers Lie Inside You.** All you need to do is look, listen, and trust.
- **Rule #10. You Will Forget All This at Birth.** You can remember it if you want by unraveling the double helix of inner knowing.

➥ POWER POINTER *Seek feedback aggressively and don't personalize what you hear. Women often take even constructive criticism as a personal affront and get their feelings hurt. This tendency goes back to the schoolyard. Whereas girls are often offended by conflict, boys can yell, scream, come to blows, walk away, and return as best buddies five minutes later. Listen to feedback analytically, and use suggestions as a challenge to improve. With this strategy, you will be less emotional and less inclined to fall into the female stereotype of crying. Tears don't solve problems. View the insights you gain from feedback as "free consulting," and strive to make good use of the knowledge you acquire. Remember, business is business. It is not personal.*

CHAPTER THREE SUMMARY AT-A-GLANCE

Use the checklist below to make sure you understand the points and steps discussed in chapter three.

Learn to be a student of the world.

☑ Use the knowledge that you accumulate daily.

☑ Stretch beyond your usual horizons.

☑ Ask probing questions.

☑ Stay current in a changing environment.

☑ Learn from everyone and everything, including negative experiences.

☑ Be a life-long learner.

☑ Build your knowledge base through reading and putting yourself in the information flow.

Use education and on-the-job training to build your knowledge base.

☑ Consider a graduate degree, if you don't have one.

☑ Get trained on the job, and/or choose a company with resources to train you.

☑ You never know what experience will be valuable later.

Seek and use feedback constructively.

☑ Seek feedback early.

☑ Internalize why you get the feedback.

☑ Find the appropriate time to dispense feedback.

☑ Identify your strengths as well as weaknesses.

☑ Take action to hone strengths and correct weaknesses.

Leadership Is Inspiring Others to Do Their Best Work

⬤ POWER POINTER *Use people skills to your advantage.*

T HE JOBS GET too big, so you have to work with and through people," comments Dawn Mello. Leadership isn't about having answers; it's about inspiring others to do their best thinking. It takes a team of talented people, working together, to accomplish important objectives. And as you rise up through an organization, you are charged increasingly with managing people and processes rather than doing the work yourself.

So, how do you build strong teams? How do you get on strong teams? And, once you're on the team, what are the keys for being a productive team member?

This chapter answers those questions with a seven-step framework for building better teams and four simple steps to be a productive team member. The steps are listed below to provide you with a sense of how they fit together.

Seven Steps to Building Better Teams
1. Choose the right leader.
2. Strategically select team members.
3. Set high standards.
4. Support the team with the right tools and training.
5. Create an environment that invites debate and encourages risk-taking.
6. Empower people by giving them a sense of ownership.
7. Show that you care.

Four Simple Steps to be a Productive Team Member
1. Do your homework.
2. Exchange knowledge with your teammates.
3. Develop a point of view.
4. Execute your responsibilities and volunteer for more if you can handle it.

Seven Steps to Building Better Teams

CHOOSE THE RIGHT LEADER

The leader influences the success of a team in so many ways. Her vision, culture, work ethic, enthusiasm, motivation, and system of reward are just a few of the myriad ways in which a leader can positively or negatively impact the success of a team initiative. Therefore, if you are in the position to choose a leader, do it with care. Consider the objectives, the skills required for success, and the personalities of everyone with whom the leader will interact—teammates and others. Make sure that the leader's

The right leader will empower people to use their judgment by giving them the confidence and support to make good decisions.

Dawn Mello

DAWN GREW UP outside of Boston, and from an early age, she loved fashion and knew she wanted to be president of a store one day. She began working in retail at the age of fifteen, and throughout her rise in the industry, she has experienced every aspect of running a store. Dawn attended a small fashion school, and after earning her bachelor's degree, she moved to New York City.

Dawn's retail career includes B. Altman & Co, New York, where she was director of fashion merchandising, and The May Department Stores, Inc. where, during a period of eleven years, she rose to vice president and general merchandise manager.

She joined Bergdorf Goodman in 1975 as vice president and fashion director, was promoted to executive vice president in 1980, and was named president in 1983. In 1989, Dawn joined The Gucci Group as executive vice president and creative director worldwide. In her fifties, Dawn leapt at the opportunity to reenergize a once-great brand. After accomplishing her objectives, and hiring her replacement, Dawn rejoined Bergdorf Goodman in 1994 as president. In 1999, she left Bergdorf Goodman and formed her own consulting company, Dawn Mello and Associates, LLC.

Dawn has been honored for outstanding achievement in her field and is a member of the board of governing trustees of American Ballet Theatre. She is single and resides in New York.

vision and objectives are in line with yours and that her style is appropriate.

The same team operating with two different leaders likely will achieve two different outcomes. That could mean varying degrees of success, or it could mean success versus failure. A strong leader will bring out the best in the individuals on your team, harnessing and harmonizing their efforts through a common vision to achieve more than the sum of the individual efforts. A strong leader will empower people to use their judgment by giving them the confidence and support to make good decisions. A strong leader creates an environment in which people are encouraged to take initiative and make decisions. In which people are not penalized for making mistakes (as long as they don't make the same mistake twice). In which people understand and believe in the vision. In which there is open, two-way communication. And in which people are treated with respect. You will succeed or fail based

B Y choosing the right leaders, Carole Black took the television station KNBC Los Angeles from a weak number-two position to the dominant number-one spot. When she started at KNBC, Black hired strong new department heads and was able to transform a demoralized group into a winning team while keeping most of the employees. She elaborates, "Everywhere I've gone, the team has become number one, and almost every time, it's a group that's already there and is considered to be composed of B and C players. The right leadership can turn things around."

on the team you put together and how you work with and through that team.

STRATEGICALLY SELECT TEAM MEMBERS

To maximize chances for success, care also must be taken in selecting every team member. The phrase "one bad apple can spoil the lot" can be applied to team dynamics. All it takes is one person, perhaps with a bad attitude, to turn a smoothly functioning team into a divisive one. Many of the same criteria apply whether one is picking a team leader or a team member. Look for people with knowledge, passion, and smarts—preferably more than you have—in the areas that are critical.

The role of a leader is to bring out the best in people, and setting high standards is an important tool to accomplish that end.

Seeking a diversity of perspectives is particularly important in selecting team members. A team is strengthened, not weakened, by having its members approach issues differently, as a more rigorous solution may be discovered if several points of view are considered. Mary Baglivo, as CEO of Euro RSCG Tatham advertising agency, sought to bring the diversity of the world into her business so that her team could examine issues through different lenses. She worked to "let self-expression happen" and then to guide her team to focus on the most promising avenues.

SET HIGH STANDARDS

Challenge people to achieve difficult goals. It is empowering. Specifically, it lets your team know that you believe they can operate at a high level and accomplish ambitious objectives. The role of a leader is to bring out the best in people, and setting high standards is an important tool to accomplish that end. Frequently individuals do not have complete information about macro objectives and their other team members to be able to accurately assess all that they can accomplish together. A leader should provide that vision.

Bringing out the best in other people requires an interest in and perceptiveness about them. Steve Jobs, founder of Apple Computer and an insightful leader, realized that Debi Coleman, who in 1981 was twenty-eight years old and controller for the Macintosh project, was capable of operating at a higher level. Coleman initially was devastated when, after six months at Apple, Jobs told her, "You are talented and smart, but you haven't really accomplished anything. I know you can do better. You haven't realized your full capabilities."

Steve Jobs saw in Debi strengths she hadn't recognized yet in herself. He pushed her to take risks, propose new ideas, and go out on a limb for the company. He nudged her to develop her skills and become a leader. After getting over her initial shock Coleman reflected on Jobs's advice and began to act. As she developed, she gained responsibility—becoming division controller in 1982, director of worldwide manufacturing in 1985, vice president of operations in 1986, chief financial officer in 1987, vice president of finance in 1989, and vice president of information systems and technology in 1990. Almost from the day of her talk with Steve Jobs, Coleman became known as a bold, out-of-the-box thinker, risk-taker, and leader. Thus, for eleven years (until Coleman's departure in 1992), Apple had an energized, effective, and visionary leader on its team—at least partially as a result of Jobs' effort to bring out the best in his employee.

Debi Coleman

DEBI, THE OLDEST of six children, grew up in a family that emphasized life-long learning. Her parents went to college when Debi was a young adult. Nonetheless, her dad worked his way up to the executive level in a manufacturing company without a degree. It was from him that she learned the ambition and drive to succeed. Debi learned social skills from her mom. The whole neighborhood "lived" at her house during her school years. As an adult, Debi carried that love of entertaining and inclination to offer thanks generously into the workplace. Thus, when her Hewlett-Packard team achieved an important success, Debi spent an entire day preparing a gourmet picnic for the group.

Debi also learned an important lesson about teamwork from one of her brothers. An avid competitor, he complained frequently about the younger kids with whom he played. One day she asked him, "If you don't like to play with Billy, then why do you do it?" He replied, "Deb, silly, it takes nine people to play on a baseball team." From that exchange, which Debi still remembers today, Debi learned that you don't have to like everyone on your team, but you do have to pull together and play your positions to win.

A liberal arts major from Brown University, Debi had a passion for manufacturing and technology, which she learned from her father and grandfather, both of whom worked for manufacturing companies. A summer job at Texas Instruments confirmed that love. Therefore, in order to supplement her liberal arts degree, Debi joined the GE financial management training program. In two years, she had four different assignments in disparate parts of the company. After that, Debi went to Stanford for her MBA. During her two years at graduate school, a summer job at Hewlett-Packard piqued her interest and led to full-time employment there, from 1978 to 1981, in cost accounting and then as a financial manager.

In 1981, Debi joined the fledgling Macintosh team at Apple Computer. During her eleven years with Apple, Coleman rose from controller for the Macintosh project to director of operations, vice president of worldwide manufacturing, vice president of operations, vice president of information systems and technology (at age thirty-two), and vice president of information systems and technology in 1990. In 1992, Debi moved to Tektronix with her mentor, becoming vice president of materials operations. When Tektronix spun off its interconnect company in 1994, Coleman became chairman and CEO. In 1999, she gave up her role as CEO of Merix Corporation but remains chairman while she pursues technology-related venture opportunities as a founding principal of SmartForest Ventures.

Throughout Debi's busy professional career, she has systematically built her leadership portfolio in the community. She has served on more than a dozen nonprofit and corporate boards during the last decade and has received approximately two dozen awards.

Debi is single and resides in Oregon.

SUPPORT THE TEAM WITH THE RIGHT TOOLS AND TRAINING

Once you've selected a team and its leader, it's critical that you provide the team with the resources for success. Those resources include not only adequate personnel but also support services, budget, the approval of top management, and training. For example, if you ask a cross-department team to develop components of a strategic plan, the team needs to understand the objectives and know that the project is important to senior management. Then you need to build in opportunity for the team members to get to know one another (if they don't already) and work on the project. Perhaps, however, not all of the team members understand the components of an effective strategic plan. One of the appropriate training steps would be to bring all the groups together for a joint session regarding issues to consider and a workable approach to developing a strategic plan. Will your team need to do market research with customers? Make sure time and budget are available. In short, give your team the tools to succeed.

CREATE AN ENVIRONMENT THAT INVITES DEBATE AND ENCOURAGES RISK-TAKING

What's the point of creating a team of talented folks with a diversity of perspectives if team members are not encouraged to express their opinions? The richness of diversity is played out in the informed debate that ensues as a team works to complete a project, map a strategy, or brainstorm a topic.

To create an environment conducive to effective brainstorming and productive teamwork, a team leader must encourage participants to feel comfortable expressing their views. In brainstorming, the whole is always greater than the sum of the parts. If each of five team members works in isolation to develop new ideas, each will operate only from her experiences and perspectives. Bring the team together, however, and each member can build on the experiences and ideas of her colleagues, thereby creating a greater number of stronger ideas.

Your employees want to contribute. Soliciting their input makes them feel valued. And when asked, they will generate terrific business ideas. When Sue Kronick sought to improve furniture delivery at Rich's, she brought together a cross-functional team that included employees from sales, distribution, and customer service. Working and brainstorming together,

In brainstorming, the whole is always greater than the sum of the parts.

they came up with dozens of interesting ideas, none of which cost the company anything and all of which vastly improved service.

Employees will support initiatives vigorously when they have contributed to the solution. Kronick could have created her own plan to improve furniture delivery and simply mandated the necessary changes. Instead, by working with her team, interdepartmental relationships were established, knowledge of the entire system was gained, and a feeling of joint responsibility for the problem and joint ownership of the solution developed. Thus, Kronick and her team both solved an immediate issue and laid the groundwork for improved service and teamwork in the longer term.

How do you encourage risk-taking and initiative by your

team? Reward it with praise and recognition. And, importantly, do not harshly criticize mistakes. Do not "kill the messenger" of bad news. Communication is critical. Focus on resolving problems, not assigning blame. And strive to help colleagues understand why errors occurred and how to be smarter the next time. Help them to evaluate their own actions for the lessons.

There is an old adage: If you give a man a fish, he eats for a day; if you teach him to fish, he eats for a lifetime. As a leader, you must give your managers the tools to be self-sufficient, initiative-taking members of your team. To do that, clearly communicate your vision and define expectations. Provide people with as much information as possible. Providing information empowers people by making them feel like they are in the inner circle and enhances their ability to evaluate circumstances and make good decisions. My husband, Bill, as president of Parkside Senior Services, was walking through a company facility when he spotted six-ounce cans of generic cola being served. That didn't seem right to him, since smaller off-price cans are used primarily in hospitals and nursing homes, and Parkside, an operator of upscale housing for relatively healthy seniors, seeks a different image. Instead of mandating a change, he discussed with the food services director why he preferred to see a twelve-ounce, name-brand soda. Afterward, the director said, "That makes all the sense in the world to me. I was just trying to cut costs." By taking the time to explain "the why" and not just "the what," Bill showed his director that minimizing costs was only one piece of the puzzle, and, in this instance, was inconsistent with the strategic vision for the company. Armed with that broader understanding, the director is better equipped to make the right decision the next time. Thus, if you help someone to understand the strategic vision and implications, she can make effective decisions. That is why strong leaders share as much information as possible, while weak managers keep it for themselves.

EMPOWER PEOPLE BY GIVING THEM A SENSE OF OWNERSHIP

In addition to empowering people through setting high standards, sharing information, and encouraging debate, there is little more powerful than providing team members with a sense of ownership. Ideally, on any project, each team member should "own" both the process and the outcome.

How do you make people feel so invested that they act like owners? First, do not micromanage the process. You have to give the team room to achieve so its members feel that it is their project. Second, encourage meaningful dialogue, and listen to what is said. If people feel that their opinions and input have been valued and have contributed to the process,

If people know that you care about them and their project, they will be more highly motivated to push for the most rigorous solution or strongest outcome.

then they will feel that they "own" a piece of it. Third, delegate to people the authority to make decisions. Then support their decision-making and initiative. That way, you prevent paralysis and keep your team moving forward. Remember, the hardest step of a thousand-mile journey is the first step. Empower your team to take that important first step.

When Pepsi needed its franchise bottlers to break a hundred-year tradition and give up their right to ship directly to restaurants, Brenda Barnes empowered those involved to help solve the problem and be part of the solution. Rather than mandate change and incur vast resistance and distrust, Barnes created a cross-functional team that included the franchise bottlers to help them see for themselves why change would be best for everyone. Ultimately, Pepsi was able to make this significant operational adjustment, not through a company mandate, but through Barnes's ability to help people choose the best path themselves and to "own the idea."

SHOW THAT YOU CARE

Showing that you care also empowers your team. If people know that you care about them and their project, they will be more highly motivated to push for the most rigorous solution or strongest outcome. Showing that you care does not require a lavish budget, but an attention to and interest in people. Sending notes requires little time and effort and is highly motivational. Especially with e-mail, it is easy to send notes to many people to let them know that you are interested in their progress or that you think they are doing a terrific job. The reason Southwest Airlines enjoys such positive employee relations and is consistently rated one of the best places to work is because the company and its leaders treat people as individuals and with respect. Colleen Barrett acknowledges any important event in her employees' lives. When she has something to share with them, she sends it to their homes, rather than to the office. She recognizes that families are part of an individual's success. Therefore, if a customer writes commending an employee, Barrett wants the family to know.

Barbara Scholley, a commander in the U.S. Navy, demands a lot from people, but she also strives to let her team know how much she appreciates their efforts. Frequently her crew is called upon to work long hours and endure seemingly endless stretches away from friends and family. The job can be intellectually, emotionally, and physically draining.

How does Commander Scholley show the team she cares? As she believes most sailors work harder than they are paid to work, she's identified four ways to reward her team. Scholley helps team members get promoted and earn more money, goes out of her way to write up people for commendations and to help them develop a strong file, gives sailors time in their schedules to study for advancement exams (thereby helping those who are so inclined and nudging along those who need it), and treats with respect her crew's family lives. For example, Scholley occasionally gives her crew a weekday off to be with their families, particularly if they've been out to sea over a weekend.

These practices are tactics we all can use to motivate a team by showing that we care. Specifically, top managers:

- Help subordinates succeed;
- Share credit;
- Promote advancement; and
- Respect personal lives.

Scholley doesn't have to work so conscientiously to support her team. In fact, her actions take considerable time and can make her job more challenging. Scholley, however, adamantly believes that showing that she cares about her team is important. As I'm sure you surmise, she is rewarded for her efforts through her team's dedication.

In 1993, Barbara Scholley was commanding the USS

Bolster with the objective of decommissioning submarines. One day, during a period of inclement weather, the cable attaching a submarine to the USS *Bolster* broke, releasing the submarine. Righting the situation was neither easy nor danger-free. When the entire crew had worked for twenty hours straight and the job still was not complete, Commander Scholley realized she needed to put divers in the water. In spite of both her crew's exhaustion and the inherent danger, she had more volunteers than she needed. The entire crew stayed with the job throughout the twenty-six-hour ordeal until the goal was accomplished. Scholley says, "In this instance, if the crew were not dedicated to getting the job done, we could have been out there a lot longer, lives could have been lost, and there might have been unpleasant personal and professional consequences. That's the kind of reward you get. By taking care of your team, they take care of you."

Recognizing and rewarding a job well done is a key strategy to show that you and the organization care. It is important not just for the current project but for subsequent ones, too. If your team goes the extra mile and you do not share the accolades and credit, then the next time that team will be far less motivated. There are a multitude of ways to reward employees, and, in fact, Bob Nelson's book *1001 Ways to Reward Employees* explores many of those techniques. Counter to what you might expect, the least-expensive rewards are the most satisfying. Start with a simple and heart-felt thank-you to each team member. Then, publicly bestow the accolades—whether in a group meeting, memo, or newsletter. Each of the techniques described above that Commander Scholley employs are essentially cost-free, yet they are meaningful. Travel opportunities and scheduling perks are other rewards that don't cost big dollars but have a motivating impact on people. Share the good assignments and glory when people perform. Celebrate the success of your teams.

Getting Onto a Strong Team

IF YOU ARE hoping to be chosen as a team member, the "likability factor" is critical—both to team selection and to success in general. Sharon Patrick notes, "All else equal, people pick the person they enjoy the most [for a team, promotion, etc.]." I've seen the "likability" point in action. At both Goldman Sachs and McKinsey, the "Pittsburgh airport test" was one tool in employee selection. Specifically, given job capability, would you mind getting stuck in the Pittsburgh airport with the person in question? If you're not sure you currently pass this test, take heart and get to work. Patrick observes, "The skills can be acquired. A sense of humor is key."

Capitalizing on people's strengths enables you to bring out the best in them and maximize their contribution to your team.

There's no way to get around it—interpersonal skills are critical to success in any endeavor, but particularly when leading or working as part of a team. Colleen Barrett, a consummate people person, employs two particularly important tactics to work successfully with others: she keeps her objectivity, and observes people's strengths and weaknesses and finds ways to capitalize on their strengths. Both of these abilities are characteristic of a strong leader or team member. Regarding the first, be fair. When personalities and other factors impinge on decisions, everyone becomes uncomfortable, team dynamics are strained, and results are impaired. However, if people respect you and your judgment, then even difficult decisions will be received better. And remember that, in this regard, perception is as important as reality. You need to be perceived as objective to be most effective.

Capitalizing on people's strengths enables you to bring out the best in them and maximize their contribution to your team—whether or not you are the leader. That involves taking time to get to know your team members and understanding what will allow them to shine. Some people are quantitatively oriented, others have great instincts, and still others have tremendous people skills. If you only give someone quantitative assignments, you may never discover what a fabulous writer she is. And if you find that person is not excelling at the quantitative tasks, then it is doubly important to probe further to find how she can best contribute. Suzanne Nora Johnson has intervened, at times, when she saw a different, more positive side of someone who was about to be fired. Many of those people ultimately became strong performers. Recognize the extraordinary human capital with which you work, and strive to make the most of it.

If you see a team that you would like to be part of, make "the ask." Don't assume others realize you would be a terrific contributing member or that you are interested. Tell them. Work to develop the relationship. A team leader will be flattered by your interest in her project. And if it doesn't work out for that particular assignment, there is a greater likelihood that it will for the next. People don't like to say no too many times. As we'll see regarding self-promotion, if you don't ask, often you don't get. Go after what you want.

Four Simple Steps to be a Productive Team Member

JUST AS THERE are identifiable characteristics of a successful team leader, there are key qualities that enable you to be a productive team member. They include doing your homework; developing an educated point of view; exchanging knowledge with your teammates; and executing your responsibilities and volunteering for more if you can handle it.

DO YOUR HOMEWORK

You must strive to do more than simply execute your assigned tasks well. Consider the entire project and how your area of responsibility fits in with the whole. Think through what questions to answer. What are the steps you and the team must take? How can you secure relevant data to begin answering the questions? Are there additional resources that should be accessed? Other points of view to explore? Have you and the team considered all the relevant stakeholders (people with an interest in the project or its outcome)? What is the anticipated result of the team achieving its objective? Where do you go from there? These are some of the key issues to consider when thinking about your team assignment. They will help you to see "the big picture" and to anticipate future issues. In short, they will help you and your team to work more efficiently and effectively.

Sheila Penrose

SHEILA AND HER older brother were raised in England by industrious parents who had high aspirations for them. Sheila's mom, who left school at fourteen, challenged Sheila to do better. Sheila's father, who left school at thirteen, nurtured Sheila, built her confidence, and ingrained in her the idea that she could do anything.

Sheila lived in an area in which only three percent of students went to universities. Her selection for higher education was a turning point for Sheila. In England, women were active in team sports, and Sheila's athletic endeavors during school provided her with important life skills such as strength, how to deal with defeat, and teamwork. Sheila received a bachelor's degree from the University of Birmingham in England and a master's degree from the London School of Economics and Political Science.

In 1977, Sheila joined Northern Trust, where she was involved in the bank's international and commercial banking services. In 1984, she attended the Stanford Executive program, and in 1985, she assumed responsibility for corporate-wide strategic planning. Sheila was appointed executive vice president in 1993 and president of corporate and institutional services in 1998.

Sheila is a board member of The Art Institute of Chicago and Leadership Greater Chicago. She is a member of the Advisory Council of Stanford Graduate School, the Chicago Club, Economic Club, Bankers Roundtable, the Committee of 200, and the Chicago Network.

She is married and resides outside of Chicago.

Taking time out to think about the issues at hand is the smartest way to begin any project. An hour up front, undisturbed, to consider the issues will enable you to craft an intelligent approach to problem-solving and can save hours or days of your time and significant money. I learned this technique from one of the most efficient problem-solvers at McKinsey. He was universally regarded as bright and a terrific team member, and yet, in an environment

> *Taking time out to think about the issues at hand is the smartest way to begin any project.*

in which most consultants worked late, he, more than anyone I knew, seemed to make time for family plus outside interests. I asked him one day about his secret to completing his work successfully while managing his workload, and he told me that whenever he had a task at hand, whether small or large, simple or complex, he thought about it before proceeding. He resisted the impulse to immediate action, and instead sat pensively until he had considered all the angles and ramifications of his task. Then he mapped the most efficient and effective path to reach his objective. His secret to working smart served his clients, his teams, and himself well and made him a popular team member and leader at McKinsey. This "secret" can help you, too.

DEVELOP AN EDUCATED POINT OF VIEW

After you have completed the research phase of your project, think through what the data is telling you. Consider the "so-what." As a consultant, I constantly analyzed data and evaluated performance, strategy, and opportunities for my client and its competitors. The data and findings, however, meant little without the "so what." So, what does the data mean? What are the implications for all relevant stake-holders? How should one act or react based upon the findings? Thinking through the "so what" provides you with another opportunity to pause and reflect on the issues and your path before again moving forward. Try never to present data to others without considering the implications and communicating the "so what."

Exchange Knowledge with Your Teammates

So, you've completed your initial tasks and you're back at the table with your teammates. How can you best advance the cause? By carefully communicating what you have learned and by listening intently to the knowledge amassed and the ideas put forth by others. Only through exchanging information will the whole team benefit from the labor of its parts. For example, teams often must choose how to allocate scarce resources. Let's say your particular group was examining how to spend limited marketing dollars to promote the sale of your product, and your assignment was to determine the viability of television as the vehicle. You couldn't make a decision about whether that was the right way to proceed without first considering the alternatives. So, the public relations expert must present her findings, and the rest of your team members must present theirs. Only then will you begin to see a more complete picture.

Being flexible in outlook and approach is critical to working successfully with your teammates, since everyone has different skills and style. By adapting your style to work best with another person, you maximize what you both can get out of the relationship. When Betsy Holden was a teacher, she learned to tailor concepts for each child. Now, as an executive, she works to adapt her management style for each colleague. Holden also learned from her children how to empower others and give them room to grow. These skills, acquired outside a business environment, help Holden to bring out the best in individuals and teams.

As president of Kraft's cheese division, Holden sat down first with the entire group and then with each individual to review what was working well and what was not working as well— regarding Holden's style and the styles of the rest of the team—and what they could do together to improve the team performance. Holden sometimes worked one on one with a team member to improve a relationship by using the Myers-Briggs analysis and then discussing the conflict areas and how best to work through them. Over a longer period of time, you learn and adapt. The basis, however, for building strong team relations is open, honest dialogue founded on trust. For only when there is trust will

THE importance of listening with the intent to understand cannot be overstated. You will be ready to listen when you realize that you don't have all the answers. Recognize that there is a great deal to be learned from others. Janet Robinson notes, "People tend to listen to their own voice too often and too long. Open your ears." And, Stephen Covey, in *The 7 Habits of Highly Effective People,* says, "Seek first to understand, then to be understood."

Suzanne Nora Johnson

SUZANNE GREW UP in Chicago, the eldest of five children in a very tight-knit family. Her father, a surgeon, exemplified using one's talents and position to help those in need and her mother (now deceased) provided strong guidance that academic, professional and commercial success could not be separated from morality and obligation. Her two sisters and two brothers are a source of tribe, stability and humor.

After graduating from the University of Southern California in 1979 and Harvard Law School in 1982, Suzanne clerked and practiced law. When she applied for a job with the World Bank, she was told she needed finance experience. Therefore, Suzanne joined Goldman Sachs. After working in the Financial Institutions Group where she worked on restructuring the Latin American debt exposure of multinational banks, Suzanne helped to found Goldman Sachs' Latin American business. In 1991, Suzanne moved to Los Angeles to head the firm's West Coast corporate finance business and she became a partner in 1992. Since 1994, Suzanne has been co-heading the firm's global healthcare business.

Suzanne serves on the Board of Trustees of the Carnegie Institution of Washington, the University of Southern California, the Harvard University Native American Program, Children NOW, Communities in Schools, and Hecel Oyakapi. Suzanne who is married, commutes back and forth between her Los Angeles home and Goldman Sachs' New York headquarters.

team members take the "risk" to honestly assess and communicate what works and what does not.

As a strong team member, you must be flexible enough to see beyond your own interests and point of view, open enough to consider many possible solutions, and adaptable enough to support the team as it moves forward to accomplish objectives. While you may be invested in your particular area of responsibility, you must get beyond that in considering the best solution. To continue the example cited above, if your job was to research television opportunities and you are the media expert, but event sponsorship was determined to be the best marketing venue, then you must accede. Perhaps, though, you'll have the opportunity to learn more about special events as the project moves forward. Being open and adaptable will enable you and your team to make good decisions and work effectively to achieve objectives.

Being open and adaptable will enable you and your team to make good decisions and work effectively to achieve objectives.

EXECUTE YOUR RESPONSIBILITIES AND VOLUNTEER FOR MORE IF YOU CAN HANDLE IT

Doing a stellar job at executing your own responsibilities and working well with your teammates will make you a valued team member. To really shine, however, you must go further. There is always more than enough work to go around, so if you can possibly handle it, volunteer for additional responsibility. In this instance, you may even be able to choose a plum assignment or a particularly interesting piece of the analysis. You'll increase your influence and importance within the team, and others will take note.

Just as you can indicate you are ready for a promotion by showing that you can do the next job, you can prove that you are ready for larger roles by taking them on. Suzanne Nora Johnson, a young vice president at Goldman Sachs when I worked with her, regularly executed her responsibilities and volunteered for more, to both the advantage of herself and her team. Not only was she thoughtful in approach and reliable in execution, but also without waiting to be asked or assigned, she consistently offered, "I'll do that analysis," or "I'll take a look at those issues." This willingness to accept more responsibility highlighted her competence, organization, team spirit, and leadership.

The flipside of volunteering for more when you can handle it is knowing when to say no when you can't. That's not easy, but it's important. Commit to what you can handle, and then do what you say. Follow through. It is better to underpromise and overperform than to overpromise and underperform.

➦ POWER POINTER *Use people skills to your advantage. Women are socialized growing up to nurture and care for others—from dolls to family members. And parents learn particularly poignant people skills while caring for their children. Recognize the value of this knowledge, and use it.*

CHAPTER FOUR SUMMARY AT-A-GLANCE

Use the checklist below to make sure you understand the points and steps discussed in chapter four.

Build a strong team.
Choose the right leader.
- ☑ Consider vision and personality.
- ☑ Recognize and build on strengths of team members.

Strategically select team members.
- ☑ Achieve team harmony.
- ☑ Seek a diversity of perspectives.

Set high standards.
- ☑ Challenge people to achieve.

Support the team with the right tools and training.
- ☑ Provide adequate resources, including personnel, support services, budget, and time.
- ☑ Make sure the team has the required training.

Create an environment that invites debate and encourages risk-taking.
- ☑ Brainstorm to find strong solutions.
- ☑ Communicate freely.
- ☑ Learn from mistakes; don't "shoot the messenger."
- ☑ Reward risk-takers.

Empower people by giving them a sense of ownership.
- ☑ Give the team room to achieve and be part of the solution.
- ☑ Encourage meaningful dialogue.

☑ Delegate authority to make decisions.
☑ Support the process.

Show that you care.
☑ Take time for little initiatives that mean a lot.
☑ Concern yourself with the success of others.
☑ Recognize and reward a job well done.

Get onto a strong team.
Consider the "likability factor."
Develop strong interpersonal skills.
Make "the ask."

Follow four simple steps to be a productive team member.
Do your homework.
☑ Consider the entire project, not just your own piece.
☑ Think through the issues so you can chart an efficient, effective path.

Develop an educated point of view.
☑ Determine the "so what" of your data.

Exchange knowledge with your teammates.
☑ Share what you've learned.
☑ Listen with an open mind to the positions of others.
☑ Be flexible in outlook and approach.

Execute your responsibilities and volunteer for more if you can handle it.
☑ Play a larger role on the team.

Problem-Solving Is an Acquired Skill

➤ POWER POINTER *Recognize the value of your experience as a woman and use that experience to problem-solve.*

"M Y ABILITY TO focus and prioritize in order to solve problems and get results has been a key to my success," observes Betsy Holden, executive vice president of Kraft.

Do you notice that your day is composed of a series of decisions that require ongoing prioritizing and problem-solving? Do you also notice that some people have a knack for working through the issues that confront them? Optimism, organization, persistence, and a creative outlook are critical to their success. Outstanding business leaders do not let themselves be derailed by obstacles. Instead, they distinguish themselves through their problem-solving.

Problem-solving can set you apart from your colleagues. Recognizing problems is important, but solving them both moves your team and company forward and reflects well on you. Your ability to clearly analyze issues and effectively solve problems is critical to moving up the ladder.

You may not realize it, but you are problem-solving all the time. Issues we confront daily range from how to prioritize our time to get the most done to how to gather key information needed for a decision. Some of us are intuitive problem-solvers, yet we can all benefit from an organized strategy. Below I've outlined a seven-step approach to effective problem-solving.

Seven-Step Approach to Effective Problem-Solving
1. Approach problems with a positive outlook.
2. Be a problem-solver, not a task completer.
3. Be persistent.
4. Use creative approaches to solve vexing problems.
5. Make decisions and move forward decisively without 100 percent information.
6. Reconcile competing points of view.
7. Push for the truth and the best solution.

Seven-Step Approach to Effective Problem-Solving

APPROACH PROBLEMS WITH A POSITIVE OUTLOOK

While it sounds Pollyannish, it's true—if you believe you can work through a situation to discover an acceptable outcome, you are more likely to accomplish that objective. As Carole Black notes, "Optimism and tenacity are a powerful combination. As long as you are smart enough to look strategically at a problem, optimism will help you reach your goal." The opposite is true as well: a defeatist attitude often leads to defeat. If you don't believe in your ability to accomplish, then frequently you will come up short. You won't have the stamina and persistence to stay with a challenge until you achieve success. Attitude, therefore, is a powerful differen-tiator—whether you are on the soft-ball field, solving a tough problem, or seeking a new job.

A fundamental confidence in your own ability to achieve will help you to do just that.

Today's most successful female leaders were raised to believe that they could accomplish anything they set their minds to. Their families ingrained this idea in them until they came to believe it themselves. Carole Black's grandfather, who lived with her when she was growing up, conveyed to her, "This is a great country. You are smart. There is noth-ing you can't do." He showed Carole, by example, how an orphaned, self-educated immigrant could become a busi-ness success. The parents of Mary Ann Domuracki and Stephanie Shern, two sisters I interviewed for this book, encouraged them to excel and treated them as though they could do anything. They were raised to believe in them-selves. A fundamental confidence in your own ability to achieve will help you to do just that.

BE A PROBLEM-SOLVER, NOT A TASK COMPLETER

When you are assigned responsibilities, it is easy to dive right into them, but it is smart not to. Instead, when con-fronted with a problem, take time out to think through the issues and how best to approach them. What are you (and your team) really trying to accomplish? Are the "tasks" on

Mary Ann Domuracki

M ARY ANN WAS born in 1954 and grew up in Taylor, Pennsylvania, with an older sister, Stephanie Shern, who also is profiled in this book. Her parents, second-generation immigrants from the Ukraine, were both active in church, civic issues, and politics—always trying to make things better. Her mom had a business degree and her dad, an accountant, earned his bachelor's and master's degrees through night and weekend classes.

Both parents treated their daughters as though they could do anything. A combination of education, talent, hard work, and belief in themselves has propelled both women to the top of their fields. Mary Ann, who started at Arthur Young like her sister, transitioned from accounting to fashion when she became chief financial officer of Danskin. After seven years, she was promoted to president and CEO. In 1998, Mary Ann became executive vice president of Kasper ASL Ltd.

Mary Ann married at twenty, but did not have her first child until she was thirty-seven. She and her husband, a consultant in the construction industry, are the parents of two grade-school children.

target to get you where you need to go? Stephen Covey advises in *The 7 Habits of Highly Effective People* to begin with the end in mind. While he is speaking in a more macro sense regarding where you want to go with your life, the same principle can be applied to problem-solving. Train yourself to first step back, consider your objectives, and examine an issue beyond its obvious attributes, then you will be able to move forward in a smarter fashion. An hour spent up front likely will save you many hours later.

BE PERSISTENT

Problem-solving requires persistence. If it were easy, it wouldn't be a problem. When Rose Marie Bravo, then president of Saks Fifth Avenue, wanted to introduce the Prada designer line into her stores as part of a nineties' strategy to offer a more upscale merchandise mix, she approached Prada's management and was turned down. Bravo, however, did not let that negative response deter her. Instead she interpreted it as "not now" and kept working to build a relationship with the Prada executives. She and her team initiated a series of conversations to persuade Prada that a relationship with Saks was in its best interests. They illustrated visual changes in their stores, arranged adjacencies with other newly acquired lines that would make Prada more comfortable, and introduced new advertising.

After a couple of years, Bravo and her team succeeded in introducing Prada into one outlying store. That success then became the basis for a larger relationship. Within eighteen months, Prada was one of Saks' top-ranking accessory brands—providing a win for Saks and a win for Prada. Bravo notes, "Never accept no. Things change—in the environment, people's perceptions, and the situation—so always seek the angles that move you toward your goal."

USE CREATIVE APPROACHES
TO SOLVE VEXING PROBLEMS

Solutions to problems often are not obvious, so don't be boxed in by traditional constraints or routines when problem-solving. Instead, employ a creative, or "out-of-the-box," approach. There are unexpected rewards to looking at things in nontraditional ways. That, too, is why the multiplicity of perspectives that results from a diverse team can distinguish success from failure.

Sharon Patrick does not allow herself to be bound by ordinary assumptions. She begins with a blank slate, or more appropriately, an empty three-dimensional space that provides her ample room to come at issues from all sides and find unique solutions. When Patrick worked at McKinsey, the firm was called upon by the federal government following the air traffic controller strike to determine why the controllers felt overloaded when management believed they were always "in the cafeteria." At first blush, the McKinsey team thought it was an organizational behavior or systems issue. Patrick, however, after mulling over the facts, realized that the situation was really a peaks and valleys traffic control issue. The spread, she observed, between the peaks (busy times) and valleys (slow periods) for controllers was

Solutions to problems often are not obvious, so don't be boxed in by traditional constraints or routines when problem-solving.

too great. This key insight enabled the government to vigorously implement flow control to smooth the curve.

Sharon Patrick has a history of "out-of-the-box" thinking. She employed both persistence and nontraditional thinking to get into Harvard Business School. Patrick had applied late, after the class of 1976 had been selected, because she hadn't even decided that she wanted to attend until only months before the start of fall classes. She had been working in government in Washington, D.C., but decided she'd prefer international business in New York, as her fiancé was moving there from abroad. However, when she applied in May 1976 to McKinsey, a firm she thought would offer international business opportunities from a New York base, she was told she needed business prerequisites.

How did Patrick employ a creative approach to solve the problem of business prerequisites? She contacted Harvard Business School, but was informed the class had already been selected and notified. As she didn't want to wait fifteen months to matriculate in the following class, Patrick inquired about admittance to the wait-list—an unusual approach to solving the problem. Naturally, she was told that it had never been done, but Patrick did not let that deter her. She asked if Harvard wanted the best people on the wait-list, which, of course, they did. Finally she wore them down, applied to the wait-list, and was admitted. Patrick's tenacity, refusal to take no for an answer, and creative approach to problem-solving enabled her to gain admission on an expedited time frame to Harvard Business School.

How can you train yourself to engage in out-of-the-box thinking? Strip away all your assumptions. Start from ground zero and "rebuild" one step at a time, challenging all

Sharon Patrick

S HARON AND HER younger sister grew up in San Diego, where the great weather encouraged Sharon's interest in sports and the outdoors—and that adventurous spirit has stayed with her. Her experience as an exchange student in Germany at age fifteen provided her with self-confidence and an interest in the world.

Sharon's father was a district sales manager for United Airlines, and he had high expectations for his daughters. He didn't accept anything less than As in school and expected them to participate in many activities. Sharon's mother was also industrious and a role model. Her talents were in the domestic arts sewing and gardening—a field in which Sharon is now employed through Martha Stewart Living Omnimedia. Even her grandmother believed women should have careers and work. Sharon was raised to be industrious.

Sharon graduated from Stanford University with a bachelor's degree in history, earned teaching credentials from San Diego State University, and received an MBA from Harvard Business School. Following her graduation from Harvard, Sharon worked from 1978 to 1989 at McKinsey, where she became a partner and founded the firm's worldwide media and entertainment practice. She also has worked on the corporate finance staff of General Motors and on the management staff of the U.S. Office of the Secretary of Health, Education, and Welfare.

From 1990 to 1993, Sharon was president and chief

operating officer of Rainbow Programming Holdings, Inc., and also was a member of the board of directors of Rainbow's parent company, Cablevision Systems Corporation. Under her leadership, the company became profitable and self-financing after twelve years of losses.

By 1993, Sharon had completed the turnaround of Rainbow and her three-year employment agreement with Cablevision. Next came the decision to leave Rainbow to "put it all together." She established her own incubator company, The Sharon Patrick Company, to allow her to apply her strategic and operating skills to projects of personal interest capable of earning her cash compensation as well as founder's equity—projects that added to her "body of work." Martha Stewart and Martha Stewart Living turned out to be Sharon's most interesting and ultimately most important client. After meeting Martha while the two climbed Mt. Kilimanjaro, Martha asked Sharon to help her—as a client of The Sharon Patrick Company—develop a multimedia business strategy and five-year plan to implement her business vision. Today, Sharon is a founder and the second largest equity shareholder in Martha Stewart Living Omnimedia, Inc., its president, and a member of the company's board of directors. With Martha Stewart, she led the team that successfully took the company public in 1999.

Sharon is a member of the board of trustees of the American Ballet Theatre, The Conference Board, the Magazine Publishers of America, the Harvard Business School Women's Association, and the McKinsey Alumni Committee. She is single and resides in New York.

that you previously have done. Zero-based budgeting refers to this approach. Jack Welch, the legendary leader at General Electric, admonishes his teams, if cost-cutting, to go for a significant reduction (forty percent, for example) rather than a small one (five percent, perhaps). While forty percent likely is not realistic, seeking such drastic change forces you to challenge all your assumptions. Therefore, by not using an "incremental" approach, you maximize your chances of finding "breakthrough" opportunities. In contrast, more traditional budgeting begins with historical and current data and extrapolates for the future. In the Sharon Patrick example above, Patrick challenged the traditional assumption that to be placed on the Harvard wait-list you must first apply for regular class admission. No assumption should be sacred.

MAKE DECISIONS AND MOVE FORWARD DECISIVELY WITHOUT 100 PERCENT INFORMATION

A key to effectiveness is to make responsible decisions on a timely basis with the information available and then to move forward. Effective leaders realize that they rarely have all the facts. Instead, they recognize when they have enough knowledge to act, and then they move forward decisively. In contrast, decision paralysis is an inability to make decisions and move forward. Decision paralysis frequently occurs when you think you can't make a decision until you have all the facts. Such paralysis renders a person ineffective. Applying the 80/20 rule, you likely can gather 80 percent of the information you desire relatively easily, however, the last 20 percent may require 80 percent of the time and effort. By the time you get close to acquiring the last details, the opportunity you were considering may no longer exist. The whole exercise, then, is worthless.

There are sociological and physiological differences in the ways men and women process information that lead to different decision-making styles—and that have implications in the workplace. Even today, women are socialized to be more communal than men. They routinely consider self plus other. In contrast, men are more self-directed and focused. Therefore, men generally are more single-minded in focusing on a goal, while women are comfortable with disparate information. Brian Sternthal, a professor of marketing at Kellogg Graduate School of Management, has done research that indicates that men focus, quickly decide an answer (often based on prior knowledge), and then block out what is contradictory or irrelevant to

Making educated decisions based upon available facts and moving forward effectively is critical to business success.

the goal. It is a top-down decision-making style. Women, in contrast, rely on stimulus and work from the bottom up. They typically examine and consider many factors before making a decision. Consequently, women are more persuadable and less certain about their decisions. The downside of the female approach is that it is not as quick, and speed can be a determinant of success. The upside, however, is that at times greater input can lead to a better decision. Therefore, recognize when speed is essential, then make the best decision with the information at hand and execute smartly.

Making educated decisions based upon available facts and moving forward effectively is critical to business success. First, you must quickly process lots of data. Second,

Mary Baglivo

MARY GREW UP in Union, New Jersey, as the oldest of four children. She was fascinated by the sense of excitement that surrounded her father's career, as a journalist for the *Newark Evening News,* and she inherited his charismatic ability to work a room. From her mom, who had an "unparalleled ability to accomplish," Mary learned tenacity, her sense of drive, and her work ethic. When Mary won a prestigious advertising award, she dedicated it to her mom. She notes, "If in her day this could have been done, my mom would have done it and made sure her daughter won, too. She was selfless."

Mary graduated Phi Beta Kappa from Rutgers College in New Jersey and earned her master's degree in advertising from Northwestern University's Medill School. She started at Tatham advertising agency as an assistant account executive in 1981, became a partner in 1986, the agency's youngest ever senior partner in 1991, president of Euro RSCG Tatham at thirty-eight, and CEO in 1998. In 1999, Mary and her family returned east to be near other family, and she joined J. Walter Thompson as executive vice president. Baglivo has won numerous awards and sits on several civic boards.

Mary and her husband, a lawyer, have two young children and share parenting responsibilities. Mary took nearly a year off from work after each child was born. Although she makes juggling work and family life look easy, she acknowledges that it is not.

use your instincts to synthesize a clear and focused point of view. And third, have the confidence, or guts, to communicate a point of view and inspire others, whether colleagues or clients, to buy into it.

Mary Baglivo does not spend much time in self-doubt, but instead trusts her instincts to make decisions and move forward. When Baglivo took over as CEO of Euro RSCG Tatham, the advertising agency was successful but lackluster. Mary felt she didn't have a lot of time to research better practices, but needed to rally her troops to produce "unexpected sparkling creative" work. By taking "ballsy" points of view and communicating with conviction, Mary and her team earned startling amounts of new business. For example, they won the Red Lobster account after competing against four major agencies. In the review, Tatham adopted an unexpected point of view and communicated it in a compelling and emphatic way: "Based upon everything we've learned about your consumer, we really think this and this alone is what you should do." What didn't they recommend? The expected. Red Lobster was famous for promoting its reasonable prices. But consumers wanted more. They wanted entertainment and escape. Tatham realized that people feel great on vacation, so Red Lobster should sell the sea, not just seafood. And with great success (and the slogan, "Escape to Red Lobster"), that's what they have done.

RECONCILE COMPETING POINTS OF VIEW

Often problem-solving involves reconciling competing demands or points of view among several parties. As you become more senior in an organization, more of your time must be spent managing people issues. Building ownership among the parties involved is an effective method of problem-solving

In 1991, when Deborah Borda was hired to be the executive director of the New York Philharmonic, the organization was shackled with a deficit of more than $2 million and faced critical contract negotiations that included the prospect of a strike. Borda successfully solved these problems by reconciling competing points of view through an approach that incorporated vision and strategy but relied upon her ability to build trust and gain "buy-in" among relevant parties. Borda established a temporary Cooperative Committee (either side could walk away after eighteen months) that included musicians, management, and the music director, Kurt Masur. The committee's mandate was to look in detail at important long-range issues and be a sounding board for more immediate concerns. Borda's positive relationship with the Cooperative Committee enabled her to communicate effectively with the Philharmonic's various constituents, to gather information, and to build trust. Further, before the negotiations commenced, she sat down with key members of the staff and board and established primary goals. Borda is a great believer in bringing people together to decide on goals. That may sound simplistic, but that's a leader's responsibility. Leaders develop strategies to achieve goals, but more importantly, they bring people together to share and buy into a common goal.

Open communication, such as that established by Borda, is a critical element in building trust and gaining "buy-in." Borda notes, "An effective chief executive officer does not control, she inspires and influences. To do that you have to provide people with the most accurate and broadest kind of information, but in a way which is digestible to them so they can figure out the different objectives."

The healthy relationship between musicians and management that resulted from Borda's efforts paved the way for many accomplishments. In 1991, the parties signed a four-year contract, which broke the cycle of three-year pacts that were often negotiated immediately following those of the Chicago Symphony Orchestra, historically the nation's highest paid. The new contract provided management with more time to both develop and implement its long-range plan and to meet the needs of the musicians. And the "temporary" Cooperative Committee, critical to Borda's strategy of building trust and gaining buy-in, is still working today and played a vital role in achieving the landmark six-year contract that was concluded in 1997. That agreement, a team effort and team success, now serves as a new model for longer-term contracts achieved without the threat of a strike. When it was concluded, the headline in the *New York Times* proclaimed, "In the Face of Strikes, A Path to Harmony." Other symphonies began calling Borda to see how she had done it, hopeful that they, too, could avert strikes—such as the recent ones in Atlanta, San Francisco, and Philadelphia—that crippled performance schedules and outraged audiences.

Push for the Truth and the Best Solution

Frequently, there are several different paths that could work to address an issue. Often, however, there is one strategy that is superior to the others. Driving to discover that strategy is important.

Deborah Borda

DEBORAH NEVER FELT any limitations in her family, which fostered an open attitude and a sense that people have a mission to seek fulfillment. Consequently, Deborah grew up with the belief that you should have an enjoyment and passion for what you do. Deborah was drawn to music, began studying at the age of six and became an accomplished violist. Deborah then attended the New England Conservatory of Music. However, she found the conservatory atmosphere stifling and left to pursue a broad liberal arts education at Bennington College. Deborah earned her graduate degree at London's Royal College of Music.

In her mid-twenties, Deborah discovered her passion for the management side of music. She gave up playing professionally, studied administration, and began positioning herself to run an orchestra. Her systematic rise through the management ranks includes serving as executive director of the Handel and Haydn Society, general manager and artistic administrator of the San Francisco Symphony, president and managing director of the Saint Paul Chamber Orchestra, executive director of the Detroit Symphony Orchestra, president of the Minnesota Orchestra Association, and executive director of the New York Philharmonic. After nine seasons with the Philharmonic, she was appointed, in 1999, to run the Los Angeles Philharmonic.

Deborah is active internationally as a lecturer and consultant, and has judged numerous music competitions.

Brenda Barnes's push for the truth and the best solution enabled her to effectively problem-solve and develop national pricing principles for Pepsi. Prior to Barnes's work, each geographic region did its own local pricing, and prices varied widely. Barnes hypothesized that there must be more science to it—that underlying pricing principles should benefit everyone. Naturally, anyone who had anything to do with pricing said, "That won't work in my market. It doesn't work that way here." However, to test her theory, Barnes did many studies of markets and pricing, including elasticity and demand curves, to come up with some "pricing truths." For example, if Pepsi is selling a sixteen-ounce bottle, it should be 89¢ (or some such set price). Barnes needed a lot of facts and convincing to get people to give up pricing autonomy, but the challenge was worth it because, in the end, Barnes believes correct pricing may have helped Pepsi beat its financial plan for four years in a row. Her push for the "best answer" paid handsome dividends.

Betsy Holden's push for the Truth and the right answer has served her well in a business environment, too.

> BRENDA Barnes, who rose through the ranks to become president and CEO of Pepsi-Cola North America, notes, "You need intellectual capability and an ability to push for the right answers and get to the Truth. Focus on finding the right solution, and don't get distracted by politics or other things. Then follow through to make sure it happens. Make the best decisions you can, and get the job done."

Betsy Holden

BETSY, WHO WAS born in Texas and has an older brother and younger sister, grew up outside of Pittsburgh. Betsy notes, "My parents taught me that if I do my best, I'll succeed. They instilled in me drive and motivation. Also, my brother taught me to pick myself up and to continuously challenge myself. Through inclusion in his world, I had male friends and developed a comfort level with men on interpersonal relationships."

Betsy, who always wanted to be a teacher, received a BA in education from Duke University and an MA in education from Northwestern University. She taught for three years, during which time she also freelanced for Playskool toy company and became enamored with business and marketing. These newfound interests motivated Betsy to return to Northwestern's Kellogg Graduate School of Management for a masters in management.

After business school, Betsy joined General Foods (now part of Kraft) as an assistant product manager in the desserts division. She has been with the company ever since and has held positions of increasing responsibility including, president of the Tombstone Pizza division, executive vice president and then president of Kraft's cheese division, and currently, executive vice president of Kraft Foods Inc.

Betsy was married during business school to another Kellogg student. They moved to New York for Betsy's job in 1982, and then back to Chicago in 1984 for her husband's job. Betsy and her husband have two children.

Specifically, she has the ability to go into a situation and figure out what it takes to be successful. When Holden ran the barbecue business at Kraft, her team won the chairman's award for superior business results. As a team, they figured out the keys to the business—pricing, advertising, and new products—and they used these levers to drive the business results. Next, Holden ran Tombstone Pizza, which already had grown from a regional to a national player in the frozen pizza market. In order to grow the business further, Holden and her team correctly analyzed the industry and determined that there was opportunity to compete with the carryout/delivery segment. Therefore, they developed DiGiorno, a self-rising pizza that successfully competes with the home-delivery segment of the market. DiGiorno has exceeded all expectations. Pushing for the optimal answer by using analysis, focus, prioritization, and action enables Holden's teams to achieve superior results.

One framework that can help you to analyze a company, product, or idea is the SWOT analysis. The concept, presented by Michael Porter in his classic book *Competitive Strategy,* refers to an analysis of Strengths, Weaknesses, Opportunities, and Threats. Strengths and weaknesses are inward-looking and refer to your own product or idea. Opportunities and threats relate to the external environment. Kraft trains its employees when problem-solving and strategizing to use its own version of a SWOT analysis. That template includes examining the following external factors:

- situation (including product quality, pricing, distribution, and new products);
- category;
- consumer;

- trends; and
- technology.

Next, you examine internally focused factors such as the product's own strengths and weaknesses. A brand manager might look at what has driven her business historically and what is likely to drive it in the future. She also would consider if there is another category impacted by an innovation that could be applied to her product/category. What has changed over time and why? What is likely to change? What can be improved?

Act decisively once you have problem-solved and reached the best solution. Execute your plan. A plan without execution is of little value. A strong leader is decisive. Indecision often implies weakness. It can confuse those who work under you and lead to inaction. When a leader makes a decision and sticks to it, that style inspires trust and provides a solid foundation on which to move forward.

POWER POINTER *Recognize the value of your experience as a woman and use that knowledge to help you specifically in problem-solving as well as throughout your job. For example, women purchase most consumer goods. So, if you work for a consumer products company, you can contribute valuable insights regarding purchasing decisions based on your own experiences. If you're a mom, your knowledge regarding kids and families can help you and your company. Companies are recognizing female purchasing power and the value of a female perspective. Use those traits and trends to your advantage.*

CHAPTER FIVE SUMMARY AT-A-GLANCE

Use the checklist below to make sure you understand the points and steps discussed in chapter five.

Approach problems with a positive outlook.
☑ Believing you can achieve your objective helps you to do it.

Be a problem-solver, not a task completer.
☑ Take time out to think through the issues before moving forward.

Be persistent.
☑ If problems were easy, they wouldn't be problems.

Use creative approaches to solve vexing problems.
☑ Employ "out-of-the-box" thinking.
☑ Challenge your assumptions.

Make decisions and move forward decisively without 100 percent information.
☑ Recognize that you rarely have all the facts.
☑ Use the available facts and your own instinct to make decisions.
☑ Act on your decisions.

Reconcile competing points of view.
☑ Build ownership among relevant parties.
☑ Maintain open communication.

Push for the truth and the best solution.
☑ Drive to discover the truth.
☑ Act decisively once you have reached the best solution.

"If a tree falls and no one hears it . . ." and Other Reasons Communication is Critical

---

> ✺ POWER POINTER *Assess your communication skills and learn to present yourself and your ideas well.*

I F YOU CAN'T communicate, you can't get anything done, in the business world or anywhere," comments Dianne Sautter, president of Chicago Children's Museum. For women in a professional environment, the issue of communication looms particularly large for two reasons. First, business language is male-oriented. Expressions, for example, are drawn from sports and warfare. Second, women are socialized to be nonconfrontational in approach and deferential in tone, which often leads to an impression of weakness. Thus, to be successful, women must recognize and respond to the fact that both their message and how they convey it are equally important.

The components of effective communication include listening and gathering information; conveying your message;

presention of yourself and your work; sales and the art of persuasion; self-promotion; having a sense of humor; and making sure there are "no surprises." These components will help you to be a strong team player and leader and aid your progress up the ladder. For, no matter how good you are, if others don't know it, then your professional development and effectiveness will be stymied.

Listen and Gather Information

TYPICALLY, WHEN YOU think of communicating, the first thing that comes to mind is talking. However, I think we should start with listening. Fundamental to a strong leader or teammate is an ability not only to listen but also to really hear. That means comprehending and contextualizing what is being said.

Strong listening skills help you in four regards. First, you learn and gather information, thereby enabling you to be wiser and make better decisions. Second, when you listen closely, you show respect for the speaker and that you value her insights.

Fundamental to a strong leader or teammate is an ability not only to listen but also to really hear.

That helps you to build a stronger relationship with the speaker. Third, and building on the first two points, listening intently encourages others to communicate with you, and, therefore, you gain more knowledge. And fourth, for those people who tend to do a little too much talking and not enough listening, remember the adage, "It's better to let people think you are stupid than to open your mouth and prove it." I put this last point in with a qualification because, as we'll see, it is important to make yourself heard. Speak up when you have a point to make, and then present it firmly. At other times, focus on listening and learning.

MAKE SURE YOU UNDERSTAND WHAT'S BEEN SAID

When someone is conveying information to you, it is imperative to understand what is being said. I learned a technique at McKinsey that both ensures that you have properly understood and assists you in internalizing the message. It hinges on repetition. After you have finished a discussion on a particular point, summarize what you have heard. While that sounds awkward, it isn't at all. Simply say, "Let me summarize what I've heard you say." That way, if you've missed a point, it will be reiterated, and if you've misunderstood, your misconception will be corrected. Also, by repeating the message, you help yourself to remember the points that have been made. If you are able to summarize the points of a conversation, then you have understood the messages.

ASK PROBING QUESTIONS

Another aspect of information gathering involves asking probing questions. Asking questions elicits answers and helps you to build your understanding and knowledge base. It also conveys an interest in the subject and the communicator that helps you to build your relationship with that person. Generally, people aren't put out by answering questions regarding an area of their expertise. Instead, they are flattered by your interest in a topic that is also of interest to them.

Being inquisitive by nature is helpful, but if you are not,

you can train yourself to systematically ask questions until you are comfortable you have drawn out all that you can from a particular story or set of facts. I can remember as a child asking my father question after question regarding some issue he had just related, until he'd literally throw his hands up and say, "That's it. I've told you everything I know." If you are not naturally comfortable asking questions, try the following exercise. As you speak to people throughout the day, try not to end a conversation without asking at least one question that provides you with additional information. Then build to asking three or four questions in a conversational fashion. This skill will enable you to draw others out and build your own knowledge, whether in cocktail conversation or at work.

When Sue Kronick first arrived on the job as president of Rich's department stores, she spent time each weekend reading all the customer mail (therefore, listening to customer comments on areas the company should be probing) and summarizing it. Similar to summarizing a conversation, summarizing customer comments ensured that Kronick was thinking about and understanding the messages. What she heard was that customers were upset regarding Rich's furniture delivery and unreturned phone calls. With that base of information, Kronick questioned and listened some more. From customers, she learned that there is a lot of anticipation about furniture. It is a big purchase and they devote time to make a decision and then take time off work for delivery. Customers, therefore, are understandably angry when something goes wrong. Kronick calculated Rich's successful delivery completion at 86 percent, leaving 14 percent of her customers unhappy.

Armed with a top-line understanding of the problem,

Sue Kronick

SUE AND HER brother were raised in the New York metropolitan area. Sue recognized her competitive spirit at an early age. She still recalls dance class in third grade, when she challenged herself to lift her leg higher than the girls around her. She also recalls her feeling of humiliation in first grade when she was put in a slow reader group. And, next to her brother, who is fifteen-months younger and brilliant, she felt that whatever she had to say was just common drivel. Sue, however, flourished when she went out on her own at Connecticut College, from which she is a Phi Beta Kappa graduate.

Sue has spent her entire career with Federated Department Stores. After college, Sue participated in the Bloomingdale's training program and went on to work there for twenty years. At Bloomingdale's, Kronick accumulated experiences in all aspects of retail and rose to senior vice president. In 1993, Sue moved to Atlanta as president and chief operating officer of Rich's, and in 1997 she was promoted to chairman and CEO of Burdine's. Sue has received numerous awards for her community involvement and serves on the board of directors of the Pepsi Bottling Group, Enterprise Florida, and Union Planters Bank in Miami.

Sue and her husband, a healthcare consultant, work hard and play hard together, and therefore elected not to have children. They reside in Miami.

Kronick queried those involved in every step of the process. She discovered that there were forty-seven hand-offs between the customer's purchase and delivery, an obvious problem. Kronick brought together distribution, customer service, stock, and sales people to brainstorm about solutions. Together, the existing employees came up with great ideas. And they banded together as a team, around the campaign "Don't drop the baby," to work toward zero defective deliveries. When Kronick left Rich's to become chairman and CEO of Burdine's, the rate of success was 97 percent. Therefore, her listening and information gathering led to an 11 percent increase in happy customers.

Don't pretend to have all the answers; ask good questions.

KNOW WHEN AND WHERE TO GET HELP

Kronick's experience illustrates another important point related to information gathering: you, personally, do not need to know all the answers. You just need to know when and where to get help. The "when" is an important judgment call, and the "where" involves accessing the appropriate resources. Don't pretend to have all the answers; ask good questions. When Janet Robinson was tapped to be president of the *New York Times,* production and labor were new areas for her. Robinson quickly figured them out, however, because she was exposed to great people who allowed her to listen, question, and learn to make insightful decisions.

Convey Your Message Clearly

IN EFFECTIVE COMMUNICATIONS, the flip side of listening and gathering information is an ability to successfully convey your message. Communication is a two-way street. You need to listen carefully, but you also need to convey your own thoughts. If you have the most wonderful ideas and valuable talents but no one knows about them, then neither you, your colleagues, nor your company will benefit.

What are the keys to conveying your message successfully? You need to tailor your content and style to your audience, keep the message as concise as possible, and organize your presentation into a logical, easy-to-follow format. Let's start with tailoring your message: Always ask yourself, Who is my audience? What is their frame of reference? If, for example, they are current college students, then citing the RTC (Resolution Trust Corporation) when discussing prudent lending practices will mean nothing without a great deal of elaboration, including a history lesson. Remember to relate to your audience's frame of reference, not your own.

Another aspect of tailoring your message for your audience involves the use of idioms and word choice. Men, who routinely use expressions from sports and warfare to make their points, dominate the upper echelons of business management. But it's only since 1977 that Title IX mandated that equal money be spent by schools on women's athletic programs, thereby increasing female exposure to sports. And women have only recently been admitted into combat in the armed services. By the next generation, expressions such as "under the gun" and "it's a slam dunk" that pepper the speech of men may be just as comfortable for women. For now, however, that's not the case. So if you are a woman in that male environment, don't be put off by these analogies. Instead, learn them, and use them if they work for you and if they are appropriate for your audience. A brief lexicon is provided below. And if you are speaking to a female audience, there may be more apt ways to make your points.

Sports and Warfare Expressions Used in Business
- It's a slam dunk (basketball) = it's easy
- It's a lay up (basketball) = it's easy
- Under the gun (warfare) = under pressure
- It's a lay down (cards) = it's an obvious winner
- Put the pedal to the metal (auto racing) = full steam ahead; give it all you've got
- Player/she's a player = she's a force to be reckoned with
- She's a team player = she works well in a team environment and doesn't hog the credit or spotlight
- Come up short = not achieve your objective
- Miss the mark = not achieve your objective
- Swing for the fences (baseball) = look for a huge impact or idea (going for a home run)
- Strike out (baseball) = fail
- Step up to the plate (baseball) = make it happen
- Be an impact player (any sport) = make a difference
- Take it to the hoop (basketball) = execute/go for the close
- Go-to guy (any team sport) = pressure player/does well under pressure
- Slugging it out in the trenches (warfare) = executing the small details
- On top of your game (any sport) = well prepared

Being concise is always better than being verbose, although it's more difficult. If you communicate concisely, there is less risk that your message will be lost on its audience. That's particularly true with memos and proposals. Focus on your main points and nail those, and they will be understood. When you are editing a memo or speech, cut out the extraneous information. Pare down to the basic facts and messages you want to convey. Eliminate extra words that do not add to your recipient's understanding or move your story forward. That sounds easy, but it isn't always. I still remember the exercise in Mrs. Hoffman's seventh-grade English class in which we read a story and then had to summarize it in one hundred words and then in fifty words. The more concise version was substantially more difficult to write. The payoff, however, is that it is easier for your audience to understand, and there is greater likelihood that they will stay with you until the end.

Organize your thoughts logically to improve your communications. One effective technique is to begin with an outline, whether you're writing or presenting a memo, report, book, or speech. An outline will ensure logical flow and adequate support for your messages. Additional organizing techniques include bullet points, charts, and graphs. There is truth to the saying, "a picture (or chart or graph) is worth a thousand words."

ORAL COMMUNICATION

Strong communication skills enhance your effectiveness and build your reputation. One-on-ones, from informal hallway discussions to formal meetings with your boss, are opportunities to gather and share information and to make a strong impression with your knowledge and communication skills. Presentations to larger groups, whether in the conference room or at industry events, provide a broader platform for accomplishing those objectives. If you are a particularly strong speaker, there may be a "multiplier effect." Many times, Sheila Penrose, president of corporate and institutional services at Northern Trust, has spoken at one event and then been invited, by someone who heard her speak, to present at another. Such opportunities build your visibility, and as you'll see, visibility is critical to advancement.

If you communicate concisely, there is less risk that your message will be lost on its audience.

Industry speeches helped Mary Ludgin build her reputation in the real estate field. Small classes at Vassar and high school training as an actress prepared Ludgin to speak at the drop of a hat and to "perform" before larger audiences. Now, whenever she communicates, Ludgin strives to figure out how her particular audience "hears" and to put her message in terms they best understand.

If you are not comfortable speaking before groups, practice that skill. Practice may not make perfect, but it sure makes better. You can practice in front of a mirror, or better yet, have someone videotape you, and then watch it. These simple, easy steps will enable you to give a more polished, professional presentation. There are numerous books on public speaking, and it is a worthwhile topic for greater exploration. Here, though, are the basics:

1. Speak slowly and enunciate. When you think you are speaking painfully slowly, it is usually just right for a

listener who is unfamiliar with your subject matter. And avoid space fillers like "um." Instead, pause if you need to.

2. Do not read your notes to a group; speak to them. To prevent the temptation to read, put your speech into outline or top-line bullet format. Then, if necessary, you can glance down, catch the point you are trying to make, and address it without reading.

3. Sustained eye contact is important. Try to maintain eye contact for a minimum of five seconds per person. That means, essentially, to finish a sentence while looking at one person before you move your focus to someone else. Rapid eye and head movement are disconcerting and do not lead your audience to believe you are focused on and speaking to them.

4. Keep your body still. Extraneous body movement, particularly shifting your weight back and forth, is distracting.

5. Appropriate gestures keep the listener involved. For example, if you are making a succession of points, count them out on your fingers. But do not point at the audience. To emphasize points, use your arms and modulate your voice.

6. And, lastly, practice. You cannot practice too much. The more you practice, the more comfortable you'll become. The more comfortable you become, the more you'll be inclined to speak out informally or to accept speaking engagements. And your reputation as a strong speaker will enhance your market value.

WRITTEN COMMUNICATION

Writing skills are part of a strong communication package. Mary Ludgin's strong written communication skills propelled her from a student in a masters in education program to CEO of a real estate company. And strong speaking skills enabled her to enhance her reputation and visibility within both her company and her industry. Ludgin comments, "If I look at the crucial moments when fate and luck came together, it was my writing and my ability to convey my thoughts that caught someone's attention." First, as a student in a masters in education program at Northwestern University, Ludgin wrote a paper that her professor loved. Two months later, a grant the professor had applied for came through and included tuition and expenses for a PhD student, so he approached Ludgin. As part of the grant, Ludgin was able to earn a master's in political science. It was this new area of interest that she leveraged to get her next job, as an urban planner in Chicago's city hall. There, a report Ludgin wrote caught the attention of JMB Realty Corporation, whose principals recruited Mary.

Ludgin's rapid advancement at JMB also stemmed from her ability to communicate effectively. After just one month on the job, a report crossed Ludgin's desk that was written by the director of research (several levels up). It was to be sent out to clients. Mary, who had not interacted with the director, believed the report was not polished enough for clients. Therefore, she took it upon herself to completely edit the piece and then walk into the director's office with "a few changes if he was interested." He was. Thereafter, he regularly chose to work with Ludgin. She was promoted to

Mary Ludgin

MARY GREW UP in a family that included a brother two years her senior and a half-sister, six years her junior. Mary learned to seek the top from her brother. She was not threatened by his many talents, but instead, chose her own arenas in which to compete and excel. She was a musician, played the oboe and particularly enjoyed solo performances.

Mary earned an AB from Vassar in 1977, an MA in 1980, and a PhD in 1988 from Northwestern University—all in political science. She has worked as an urban planner for the City of Chicago and in retail site location for a supermarket. In 1990, she joined JMB Institutional Realty Corporation and served as vice president and director of research. When the firm was purchased by Heitman Capital Management in 1994, she became a managing director and director of investment research at Heitman. In 1997, she was named COO and in 1998, president and CEO. Mary now is responsible for running a 60-person firm with $6.7 billion in assets under management.

Mary married at 38 and adopted a baby girl a few years later. She notes that before she married and became a mom, she had fewer competing demands and found it easier to work nights and weekends. However, she always has tried to create a climate in which men and women feel comfortable juggling family and work responsibilities. She and her family reside in Illinois.

vice president within two months and a terrific partnership ensued.

COMMUNICATE EFFECTIVELY IN A MALE-DOMINATED BUSINESS WORLD

Presentation counts. It's not just what you say but how you say it. If you don't communicate correctly, your entire message may be lost. Or, you won't get the credit.

Women tend to communicate differently than men, and in a business world still dominated by men, the female approach often is less effective. Whereas women are socialized growing up to "fit in" and popularity comes from conforming, boys are respected for standing out, whether on the playing field or in the classroom. Now carry those tendencies to the conference room. Men tend to boldly state their opinions and vie to be heard. Women, not wanting to stand out or risk offending anyone, rarely make strong statements. They often present their ideas with caveats, are meek in tone, and are deferential in style. Consequently, the same idea, presented by John and by Jane, may be heard differently by the group at that conference table. John gets credit for a bold idea, and no one remembers Jane saying much of anything. While this description involves many generalizations, it is, unfortunately, too often real. That's the bad news. The good news is that the communication gap between men and women is narrowing. Every day, there are more and more women in positions to mentor who recognize the rules of effective business communication and labor to share them with their female colleagues.

What can you do to communicate most effectively?

Susan Getzendanner

$\begin{smallmatrix}S\end{smallmatrix}$USAN WAS BORN in 1939 as the second of six children and grew up in Chicago. She and her siblings are the first generation in their family to attend college, and each now has two degrees (her brother has three). Susan's dad was a salesperson and her mom a housewife. Her mom, however, encouraged her girls not to be housewives, as she found it boring.

Susan attended an all-girls high school, where she was a class leader, editor of the paper, and volleyball player. Susan then went to Marquette College and Loyola University Law School, where there were 2 women out of 120 students in her 1966 class (now classes are approximately 50 percent female). Nonetheless, she quickly established herself as a leader and graduated first in her class.

Susan has been a trailblazer throughout her career. She was the first female partner at Mayer, Brown & Platt and, in 1980, the first woman to be named a federal judge in Illinois. She currently is a partner at Skadden, Arps, Slate, Meagher & Flom (Illinois). She is a member of the Commercial Club, the Economics Club, and the Chicago Network; a director of Urban Shopping Centers, Inc., the Rehabilitation Institute of Chicago, and numerous public interest organizations; and is considered one of Chicago's top trial lawyers. She has been named in the *National Law Journal*'s first listing of the fifty most influential women lawyers in America.

Susan is married and has two grown children.

Susan Getzendanner, a leading attorney and past federal judge, advises young female lawyers to do the following:

1. never apologize;
2. shake hands firmly;
3. speak confidently and with strong intonation;
4. make statements rather than ask questions; and
5. make your presence felt and your voice heard.

Let's discuss these points. First, never apologize. Getzendanner notes that this piece of advice stems from years of watching women behave. She observes that frequently when a woman stands up in a meeting she begins with an apology—for her voice, a cold, being late, and so on. Getzendanner, in contrast, does not apologize for anything. She goes so far as to advocate, "Never admit you are wrong." Deborah Tannen, in her informative book *Talking from 9 to 5*, also recognizes women's tendencies to apologize. She suggests that the apology is offered only as a figure of speech—to make others feel comfortable—but it has the effect of putting the woman in a "one-down," or weaker, position. The next time you have an urge to apologize in a professional setting, try to move on without it.

A firm handshake conveys confidence and provides important symbolism in business. When you are introduced to someone, look him or her straight in the eye and say hello, while shaking the person's hand firmly. A limp handshake can be so negative that it is a turnoff.

Your tone of voice when you present your ideas communicates a great deal of information. A firm, confident tone is much more persuasive than a weak, indecisive one. A strong voice conveys your belief in what you are saying, and that confidence will be contagious to others. If you show that you believe, there is a greater chance that your audience will, too. Specifically, avoid the sing-song intonation that ends each phrase on the up and makes statements sound like questions; enunciate, speak professionally, and state your message with authority. Strong intonation and confident body language are critical to successful communication.

Make your presence felt and your positions heard by communicating thoughtfully, not emotionally.

Similarly, when you want to make a statement, make a statement; don't present your statement as a question. Jane might say, so as to include everyone in her thought, "Shouldn't we consider this?" John, in contrast, will say, "Let's do this!" Who do you think gets credit for the idea? Of course, it is John, who forcefully presented his suggestion as "the way to go."

Make your presence felt and your positions heard by communicating thoughtfully, not emotionally. Women often are perceived to be emotional, and that may be held against them in a professional environment. In a business world, decisions should be made based on facts, not emotions, so a measured approach works best. For example, Indra Nooyi, senior vice president of corporate strategy and development for PepsiCo, might say, "I heard all your points of view and they are all strong, but I've been a strategist for seventeen years in many different environments for fifteen different companies and have had a chance to see what worked and what did not. Based on this experience, I believe we should. . . ." With that statement, Nooyi is forcefully on record for what she believes. She has taken a stand and ensured that she is heard and counted.

Going on record is important. Women don't like to say the obvious, especially if it already has been said in a meeting. But you need to go on record for yourself. Making yourself heard helps you to be perceived as a valuable team player or leader and will ultimately help you to distinguish yourself from among a crowded field of talented colleagues. Barbara Scholley learned to project her voice and push her way into conversations in her roles in the United States Navy. Having been raised that girls are sweet, while boys can be bullies, Scholley worked to be more assertive to ensure that she was heard.

How you go on record also counts. Suzanne Nora Johnson has spent years working with men and women in the predominantly male environment of investment banking. Based on that experience, she notes, "I have seen women held back for stylistic not substantive reasons, and it's frustrating. You need to be aware of the criteria and adjust your style to be comfortable on a male scale, too. Most women think the standards are objective, but there is a huge qualitative piece—for example, the way you speak. There is a fine line between being forceful and assertive, while still maintaining your femininity."

How can you be forceful, yet feminine? Adopt a thoughtful, measured approach, such as that employed by Indra Nooyi in the example above. Speak articulately and with little emotion. Give your point of view even if you think it already has been said. Be strong. Be compelling. And deal with hard as well as soft issues. That means if you are evaluating a company, don't just discuss the human resource issues. Address the numbers—the sales and profits—and the nuts and bolts of the business. Show that you are informed and articulate regarding traditionally male fields, too.

Being forceful as a woman can expose you to the stereotypical slight, "she's so aggressive." The equivalent man, however, would be admired for his assertiveness. This dichotomy illustrates the narrower band of acceptable behavior for women. This narrower band, discussed further in chapter nine, was experienced and referenced by many of the leaders I interviewed. And it is one of the central reasons why it's more difficult for women than men to succeed in a traditional business environment.

Personal Presence and Presentation Count

YOUR PRESENCE AND presentation speak volumes about you to your colleagues, clients, and customers and are key to selling an idea, earning new business, or getting others to take note of your abilities. Presence includes your posture, your voice, your appearance, and your comportment—so stand as tall as you can, speak as firmly and with as much conviction as you can, take care to be as well groomed as you can, and be as professional as you can.

PERSONAL PRESENTATION

Attire is one of the most visible aspects of your personal presentation and grooming. For women, attire is more complicated than for men, as men typically stick to a "uniform" that does not distinguish them based on dress code. In formal business environments, that means a suit and tie, and in casual offices, it implies khakis and a collared shirt. For women, the range of attire is broader and, therefore, trickier.

How can you ascertain what is the most appropriate business attire? Follow the lead of those who are well regarded and more senior than you. That means emulating those one or two levels up. Also, dress to draw attention to the professional, not the personal. Think about whether you want people to focus on your message or the fact that you are a woman. If it's the message, then dress down the woman side. No big hair, big jewelry, big nails, small skirts, thin blouses, or high heels. When Indra Nooyi first started at PepsiCo, she watched some women in a meeting, and then watched the men watching them. Afterward, she asked the women, young Wall Street recruits, what they wanted to draw attention to—their hemline or their contributions? Initially, they responded with resentment, but soon got the message.

Remember, too, as you rise up in an organization, you become a role model for others. Barb Allen was always conscious that she set the tone for women at the Quaker Oats Company. In the eighties, Allen went out of her way to wear professional pantsuits so others would have a comfortable alternative to skirts and pantyhose.

When Veronica Biggins began wearing maternity clothes for the second time (she was expecting her second child) at Nations Bank, colleagues thought she was crazy and wondered if she was giving up her career. When she didn't quit her job, maternity clothes began appearing throughout the bank, as people saw that it was okay. Note that I've used "maternity clothes" here as a metaphor for pregnancy. But had I said "pregnancy," the point would've been the same:

Veronica Biggins

WHEN I ASKED Veronica what in her upbringing prepared her for success, she responded, "Having great parents and a great education." Veronica was raised in South Carolina in the 1960s and attended segregated parochial school. The Biggins family emphasized education by word and example. Veronica's mom finished college when Veronica was in high school, and then went on to complete a master's degree and teach. Her father had a master's as well and chaired an engineering department. The Biggins children followed their parents' lead: Veronica earned a bachelor's degree from Spelman College and a master's degree from Georgia State University; her older and younger brothers also have two degrees each.

Veronica began her twenty-year banking career as a management trainee at the Citizen and Southern Bank and rose through the ranks to become executive vice president for corporate community relations at Nations-Bank, which had acquired Citizen and Southern.

Veronica left banking to join the White House as assistant to the president and director of presidential personnel, where she was responsible for the selection and hiring of political appointees within the federal government. Following her time in D.C., Veronica joined the Heidrick & Struggles executive search firm in Atlanta as a partner. She serves on several corporate and trustee boards.

Veronica is married and has two teenage daughters.

as you gain seniority, you become a role model for more and more people. Therefore, set the right tone through your actions and presentation.

How you comport yourself sends subtle but powerful messages about where and how you "fit in" to an organization. The objective in a professional environment is to act professionally. That entails obvious behavior such as not chewing gum in meetings and not biting your nails, but it also can be more subtle, such as not falling into gender stereotypes. Therefore, don't get the coffee unless it's in your job description. Gender stereotypes do not help you, so don't contribute to them. I learned that lesson in my first week of work at Goldman Sachs. It was late, and I joined a dozen colleagues in the conference room for some order-in Chinese food. As I finished, I rose to clear my paper plate and instinctively started to pick up someone else's (especially damning since it was a male colleague's). I was raised, after all, to be polite and "pitch in." Suzanne Nora Johnson gently pulled me aside and said, "Don't pour the coffee, and don't clear the plates. Let everyone— the guys especially—fend for themselves. You don't need to serve." I understood the message at once.

In a professional environment, you want to be seen only as a professional—a professional investment banker, for example. You do not want to be cast in a support or sub-servient role. More than a dozen years later, I interviewed Suzanne for this book and we reminisced about that lesson. She said that just that day she had had a similar experience. She stopped a young female colleague from cutting some birthday cake for the group with the suggestion, "Let the doctor do it." The implication was that a former doctor (and male colleague in the room) might have more cutting experience. The real message to the female banker, however, was: Don't fall into the role of serving others. She understood immediately.

PRESENTATION OF YOUR WORK

As with your own personal presentation, the appearance of your work often leads to an important first impression. I used to think that formatting a document was window dressing and relatively unimportant versus content. But if my audience can't easily comprehend my content, then the entire message is lost. Therefore, time spent organizing your presentation, whether verbal or written, whether to one person or to many, is critical. Outlines, bullet points, graphs, and diagrams are terrific tools for organizing and communicating your thoughts.

Attention to detail regarding presentation has an additional benefit: it conveys that you care about your work.

Attention to detail regarding presentation has an additional benefit: it conveys that you care about your work. Sloppy appearance, in contrast, gives the impression that the work itself is sloppy and not important to you. These messages inhibit the success of your efforts. Beautiful presentation, however, is no substitute for strong content. Rather, it is the icing and the filling, once the cake has been baked. If you want someone to bite into it, make sure it looks appealing, and then deliver on taste.

Sales and the Art of Persuasion

YOU ARE SELLING all day long. Whether or not you realize it, when you make a suggestion or put forth an idea, you
are selling. You also are selling when you go for an interview.
The product is you. And, of course, when you make a traditional sales call, you are selling a product or service. Even
when you think you are not selling, you are, because you are
always making an impression. Whether you are at a cocktail
party, the grocery store, or a sales call, recognize that the
impressions you make feed your reputation, which has a
direct impact on your ability to sell. Selling is integral to success, and communication is integral to selling.

Janet Robinson, the president and general manager of
the *New York Times* newspaper, succeeds in selling ideas and
products because she knows what she's up against. First, she
does her homework regarding a client's objectives before the
sales call. She is prepared. Second,
she is cognizant of a client's time.
Her preparation enables her to cover   *Selling is integral to*
ground expeditiously in a meeting,   *success, and communica-*
and she follows up quickly with pro-   *tion is integral to selling.*
posals and other information. Third,
Robinson builds relationships over
time through associations that serve the newspaper industry,
including Women in Communications, the Ad Council, and
the American Advertising Federation. Such community involvement enhances existing relationships and helps you
build new ones by giving others a good feeling about both
you as a person and your organization. Robinson builds her
relationships based on trust. Her clients know she will stand
up for them. Finally, Janet is continually cognizant of the fact

that she is always making an impression and works to make it positive.

Success in sales requires many of the same qualities as success in any business endeavor—passion, hard work, persistence, and creativity. Your enthusiasm for your product or service is contagious and will infect your clients and customers. So, where possible, put yourself where you can be passionate about what you sell. Hardwork also makes a difference. Valerie Salembier, in her myriad sales-related jobs in publishing, made her sales calls during the day and did her administrative and creative work before and after hours. Sales requires commitment.

Sales also requires patience and persistence. It takes time to build relationships with people so that they trust you and want to do business with you. At *Ms.* magazine, Salembier pursued an airplane manufacturer for two years before "land-

Y OUR power is limited only by your power of persuasion," notes Sheri Wilson-Gray. She learned through experience the importance of sales and brokering deals. Specifically, Wilson-Gray found that intellectual horsepower is 50 percent of accomplishing an objective—for example, putting together a good plan. The other, perhaps more important piece is selling it. Wilson-Gray also learned from her work on some of Procter & Gamble's smaller brands that you really need to work the system and your colleagues to get things done. Then when you do a deal, it sticks. Sheri says, "It's not what you market that matters, but that you market."

ing" the business. When she finally got in to see the decision maker, her enthusiasm for her product carried the day, and she sold six pages, an impressive spread. Why, you may be wondering, did Salembier target an equipment manufacturer for *Ms.*? Because they were advertising prolifically in thought leader publications. Knowing that, when Salembier made her pitch, she said, "If you are looking for people who call up and ask what airplane equipment they fly, you are missing an activist audience that *Ms.* can provide." Salembier had done her homework.

Sales also requires "out-of-the-box" problem-solving. You must think creatively about your potential customers and how to engage them. At *Newsweek* twenty years ago, Salembier sought a watch account the magazine hadn't been able to secure. To engage the potential client, Salembier interviewed people on Park Avenue in Manhattan regarding what type of watch they wore and why. The client loved the tape, and *Newsweek* ultimately won the business.

Self-Promote Gracefully

SELF-PROMOTION IS a vital facet of communication because it's the area in which you convey to others your capabilities and experience. It is a form of sales, but it must be done tastefully, subtly, if you are not in an interview situation. Although self-promotion is a critical piece of success, it's an area that many women find uncomfortable. Discomfort, again, stems from the socialization that teaches girls and women to shrink from the spotlight and blend in with

Today's leaders know that self-promotion is key to effectively rising up a corporate ladder.

others. Women often learn, overtly and by example, to be more demur and soft-spoken. Self-promotion requires a certain brashness that is more consistent with the way boys are raised. While you should seek a style that is comfortable to you, you must let others know what you can do.

Today's leaders know that self-promotion is key to effectively rising up a corporate ladder. People need to see what you do to recognize it. Too often, women believe that if you do the right thing, you'll be rewarded. Such thinking is analogous to the old question about the tree in the forest: If a tree falls and no one is there to hear it, does it make a sound?

SIGNAL YOU ARE READY FOR A PROMOTION

How can you utilize self-promotion to signal that you are ready for advancement? Share with your boss the next six things you are thinking about in regard to your business rather than the last six things that you did. This technique shows that you are assessing how to take the business to the next level, which is a key to promotion. Another compelling signal is to take on, whenever possible, responsibilities associated with that next level.

"Reality is reality, and perception is, too. People have to feel comfortable promoting you," comments Carole Black, the president and CEO of Lifetime Television. Focusing on achieving in her current job and presenting herself so others think she'll fit the next position has helped Black in her quick ascent through the media world. What specifically did Black do to get people comfortable? She strove to go above and beyond what was expected. She was proactive—particularly in terms of coming up with new ideas and creative ways of thinking. She showed that she was willing to take on extra responsibility. And Black proved her leadership ability through mentoring others. These techniques proved to Black's colleagues that she was capable, conscientious, and committed. And they made her superiors comfortable that she could handle additional responsibility.

You can't count on the fact that your capabilities will be noticed, so if you have real results to show, find someone further up the food chain who will appreciate them and then share without being obnoxious. For example, over coffee, you might say, "I was reviewing the numbers and came across something amazing. . . ." Be sure to complement the team that did the work. People respect someone who has the confidence, grace, and leadership skills to share credit. Another technique is to do "catch-up" meetings with your boss. Valerie Salembier routinely asks for fifteen minutes to review a couple of things. Then she is able to show her team's progress or discuss issues that have arisen. She not only gains helpful feedback and builds her relationship with her boss, but she also showcases her own leadership and team initiatives.

> *People respect someone who has the confidence, grace, and leadership skills to share credit.*

STAY IN TOUCH WITH THOSE IN POWER

You need to be in touch with people who are in power. Just sitting in your office doing a great job isn't enough. Janet Gurwitch Bristow learned this lesson early in her career through a painful experience, but thereafter it helped her to be more savvy and progress more quickly in navigating

ONE day, when Sue Kronick was a vice president and merchandising manager at Bloomingdale's, she ran into Howard Goldfeder (then chairman and CEO of Federated, the parent company of Bloomingdale's), who asked her how she was feeling. Kronick replied, "Since you asked, I think I could be moving faster." Ten days later, she was offered a GMM position and senior vice president title—a huge promotion. You may be thinking, what good fortune for Kronick to have run into Howard Goldfeder. Well, it wasn't an accident. Sue knew Goldfeder was in town, and so she made it her business to be on the management floor. That's making your own breaks.

corporate waters. At Foley's department stores, Gurwitch Bristow was told in a review that she was the strongest performer of a hundred people at her level. However, six months later she watched with shock and disappointment as another woman was promoted to the divisional level. When she approached the general merchandise manager (GMM), who was two levels up, she was told, "I've never seen you." Sixty days later, with her profile raised, she was promoted. Janet feels the promotion wouldn't have happened if she hadn't gone to the GMM. She concludes, "You need to be politically aware—if not savvy—and let people know who you are."

How can you self-promote with grace? Take advantage of natural occasions. For Gurwitch Bristow, it was natural for her, as a buyer (low to mid-level) at Foleys, to be with her boss, the divisional and the GMM on a market trip. Gurwitch Bristow prepared carefully for those opportunities to show what she knew and could do. She notes, "It is usually the buyer's job to plan the day, so plan it to show your skills. And use elevator time with your colleagues well. That way, when the GMM puts together a Buyer Advisory Group, you are considered."

MAKE "THE ASK"

A corollary of the critical self-promotion axiom is: If you don't ask, you don't get. That corollary applies to terrific assignments, promotions, and compensation. The squeaky wheel does get the oil. For all the same reasons cited above, women are less comfortable asking for jobs, promotions, and dollars. Linda Hoffman, managing partner at Coopers & Lybrand, commented in a *Business Week* magazine article that, until she was in senior management, she would never have imagined the tremendous difference between what men and women ask for—or do not, as the case may be. In general, men are far bolder. They not only routinely ask for promotions and raises—far more often than do women— but also rate themselves higher on self-evaluations. These facts alone can account for some of the disparity between rates at which men and women rise in the workplace.

Making "the ask" helped propel Carole Black to the next level when she was at Disney. As she had been successful building Disney's home video business, she was approached to run their television unit. At the time she was tapped for the new job, Black was a vice president, but aspired to be a senior vice president for two reasons. First, there were no women senior vice presidents. Second, being a senior vice president made her a part of the core management team. Thus, Black responded to the opportunity by communicating that she'd accept the new position if she were made a senior vice president. And she was. If Black hadn't asked, she never would have received the more senior status and title.

One of the "asks" that women are reluctant to make is for more money. Women currently earn seventy-six cents for every dollar men earn. In 1970, women earned less—just seventy-two cents for every dollar their male counterparts took home. While the trend is in the right direction, progress has been slow. As women gain the confidence and comfort to push for increased compensation, the wage gap will narrow.

In the business world, worth is often measured in dollars, so you need to pick the right strategic moments to make your play for what you are worth. When Sue Kronick was promoted to manager from assistant manager, an entry-level position at Bloomingdale's, she was offered a five-thousand-dollar raise. Kronick responded to her boss that she required ten thousand dollars because she would need a car to visit the stores. Her thinking was that if she didn't have a car, she'd have to take the bus, but then she wouldn't be able to stay late, so she wouldn't be positioned to succeed. Women don't often tie their performance to monetary value the way men do. It's okay to ask. Just choose your moments wisely.

Have a Sense of Humor

AS WE SAW in the discussion on team building in chapter four, all other things being equal, people choose for an assignment or promotion someone with whom they enjoy working. Humor is an important element contributing to the rapport between two people. Humor puts people at ease. It helps in many areas, including communication. If people feel comfortable, they tell you more. If you are listening, you'll learn more and do better. Sue Kronick cites her spontaneous sense of humor and her resulting ability to put people at ease as one of the keys to her success. When she arrived at Burdines as chief executive officer, she knew her predecessor had a casual style around the office and frequently removed his shoes. Therefore, when Kronick made her first presentation to two hundred employees in her stocking feet, the audience roared. Thus, she was able both to let employees know that she understood how things worked and to diffuse some of the natural tension that occurs in a leadership transition. She summarizes, "If you take yourself too seriously, it's not fun for people. I'm in the retail business; that's not life or death."

Make Sure There Are No "Surprises"

THIS IS A quick point, but an important one: When you communicate can be as important as what you say. People don't like surprises, especially in a business environment. That means sharing good news as well as bad. If you hide something, it won't disappear; instead, it's going to explode in your face in a bigger way. It takes courage to do so, but if there's a problem at work, let your boss know. She then can (1) help to solve the problem and (2) prepare other parts of the organization for the impact of that issue. By keeping the lines of communication open at all times, and especially when difficult issues arise, you actually are helping your boss to succeed in her job, thereby helping yourself as well.

Setting realistic expectations will help you to avoid

Valerie Salembier

VALERIE WAS BORN in New Jersey, the younger of two girls in a competitive, sports-minded family. Her mom adopted a "take no prisoners" approach to whatever she did and mastered everything she went after.

After graduating from the College of New Rochelle, Valerie began her publishing career at Time, Inc., as a secretary, and became the first woman hired onto the advertising staff at *Newsweek* magazine. At *Ms.* magazine, she rose in six years from advertising sales director to associate publisher. Valerie's subsequent publishing posts have included: senior vice president of advertising for *USA Today*, publisher of *TV Guide*, president of the *New York Post*, publisher and senior vice president of the New York Times Company's *Family Circle*, vice president of advertising for the *New York Times*, and since 1996, publisher of *Esquire*.

Valerie has received numerous awards. She is a trustee of the New York City Police Foundation and created that organization's Businesswomen's Roundtable to provide accomplished business mentors to high-ranking women in the NYPD. She is a board member of the National Alliance of Breast Cancer Organizations, B.O.X. (the Beneficial Organization for Ex-fighters), Central Synagogue, and the New York City Sports Development Corporation. Valerie is a member of the Committee of 200, the Women's City Club, the Women's Forum, and Women in Communications.

Valerie is married and has two stepchildren.

surprising people. It is far better to underpromise and over-perform than the reverse. Then, if results don't match expectations, people will be pleased rather than disappointed. Of course, being as accurate as you can in your assessment of what you (and your team) can do in a given time frame is best. Don't let yourself be tempted to set an overly ambitious deadline for your team or an overly aggressive statement of what you can accomplish. The momentary "credit" that you receive will long after be displaced by the liability accorded your "account" for failing to deliver as promised.

Conversely, if something surprises you, that surprise can reverberate throughout your organization. How can you lessen your chance of being surprised? Anticipate. Think ahead. Valerie Salembier learned this lesson the hard way, and now trains herself to anticipate. When Salembier worked at *USA Today,* she once filled in for her vacationing boss at a management meeting with Al Neuharth, the owner of parent company Gannett. Kellogg's Cornflakes had made a significant advertising commitment to *USA Today* that culminated in an eight-page spread in the July 4 edition. It was the largest advertisement ever run by one company. Consequently, in the meeting, Neuharth turned to Salembier and asked, "So Val, when you called the president of Kellogg this morning to see if he liked his advertisement, what did he say?" Salembier took a deep breath and replied, "Al, I haven't called him yet." From that moment, she vowed to do a better job anticipating. Now, when Salembier occasionally finds she hasn't anticipated as well as she'd like, she writes the word "anticipate" on an index card and leaves it on her desk for the next month.

Anticipating the needs of your superiors and clients will help you succeed in business. Mary Ludgin has always tried to figure out the personal style of her boss and work to it. If her boss liked to reserve 8 to 9 A.M. as a quiet time before a hectic day, then Mary would stop in to provide an update or transact what she needed to get done at 6 P.M., after the crush of business ended. Additionally, if she perceived (that is, anticipated) that her client would feel more comfortable knowing three days before a report was due that it was on the way, Mary would call and say, "Just wanted to follow up and let you know it's coming." Anti-cipating the needs of others is important anywhere, including at work.

POWER POINTER *Assess your communications skills and learn to present yourself and your ideas well. Communication is the area where women frequently have to work hardest to over-come a lifetime of socialization that teaches them to avoid con-flict, directness, and self-promotion. How you present yourself and your ideas makes a difference in how you are perceived, whether you get credit for an idea and whether you are viewed as a winner. Take time to assess your communication skills, and get help if you need it. Generally, organizational resources are available if you ask, and colleagues are happy to help. Your interest in your own self-development will enable you to build skills, and your drive will convince others that it is worthwhile to invest in you.*

Remember, sitting in your office doing a great job isn't enough. Your colleagues need to recognize your capabilities and contributions. Self-promotion, which is difficult for many women, can make a difference.

CHAPTER SIX SUMMARY AT-A-GLANCE

Use the checklist below to make sure you understand the points and steps discussed in chapter six.

Listen and gather information.

☑ Listen intently to gather information, show respect for the speaker, and encourage others to communicate with you so that you gain additional knowledge.

☑ Summarize what you've heard to ensure that you understand the message.

☑ Ask probing questions to elicit additional information.

☑ Know when and where to get help so that you don't have to have all the answers.

Convey your message clearly.

☑ Tailor your content and style to your audience.

☑ Be concise.

☑ Organize your presentation in a logical, easy-to-follow format.

☑ Speak with aplomb.

☑ Write persuasively.

Communicate effectively in a male-dominated business world.

☑ "Never" apologize.

☑ Shake hands firmly.

☑ Speak confidently and firmly (no sing-song voice).

☑ Speak logically, not emotionally.

☑ Make statements rather than ask questions.

☑ Make yourself heard.

☑ Address tough issues.

Your personal presence and presentation count.

☑ Dress, groom, and comport yourself for professional success.

☑ Present your work with care.

Practice sales and the art of persuasion.

☑ Recognize that you are selling all day long.

☑ Learn the sales secrets—know what you are up against; be perceptive; be prepared; build relationships with key clients.

Practice self-promotion.

☑ Show your boss the next six things you are thinking about in regard to the business.

☑ Present yourself so others think you'll fit the next position.

☑ Share your results and efforts.

☑ Stay in touch with people in power.

☑ Self-promote gracefully and naturally.

☑ Make "the ask."

Have a sense of humor.

☑ Make people feel comfortable.

Avoid surprising people with information.

☑ Keep lines of communication open.

☑ Set realistic expectations.

☑ Anticipate.

The More People You Know, the More You Can Get Done

⟶ POWER POINTER *Women-to-women connections work.*

J UST AS MONEY is tangible currency, relationships are intangible currency. Relationships are how and why most things get done in business and in life. Relationships determine who receives a particular assignment or promotion, who earns a piece of new business, who is selected for a board, and much more. Your day-to-day interactions with people, whether in a conference room, supermarket, boardroom, or health club are critical to your success. Building broad networks and developing strong ties with mentors and sponsors are particularly important aspects of relationship-building. It is also wise to avoid burning bridges.

Networks

IN RECENT YEARS, the term "networking" has acquired negative connotations, conjuring up visions of "eager beavers" rapidly handing out business cards as they anxiously work to

163

climb the corporate ladder. While dispensing and collecting business cards alone does not create a relationship, working or talking with someone, so that you learn about each other, can.

How Networking Helps You

Everything gets done through people, so the broader your network, the more you can accomplish. Specifically, networking helps you to gather information and build your expertise, generate business, help others, accomplish large objectives, do your job efficiently and effectively, and even land your next position. Marilyn Lederer elaborates, "Men do business on the golf course and in the sky box at sporting events because that's where their networks are. Women are learning. Meeting one person and then another has been the basis for my career." Below, I share with you examples that bring to life the value of developing your own network. Then I'll show you how to create or expand yours.

Networking helps you to gather information and build

> Networking is critical," comments Connie Duckworth, managing director at Goldman Sachs and CEO of MuniGroup.com. "The term is a fancy word for developing a series of smaller relationships. It's every time you work with someone, getting to know them and how you may access them or be accessed in the future. The relationships are gradually acquired over time; little by little, as you work with people, your network expands."

your expertise. When the leadership team at Chicago Children's Museum began plans to raise $15 million to triple in size and move to a permanent home, there were many questions to be answered. What should be projected in terms of visitors, admissions, and family memberships in years one through five? How should admission and membership be priced? What systems should be installed? What range of grand opening events would welcome the museum's many constituents while maximizing revenue and public relations opportunities? And how should the museum prepare for any potential controversy around a cutting-edge exhibit dealing with the tough topics of prejudice and discrimination? These were just a few of the myriad issues to be explored, and each was resolved through extensive research that utilized networking at its core.

Everything gets done through people, so the broader your network, the more you can accomplish.

To figure out what Chicago Children's Museum could expect for admissions and memberships in its new facility, I called my colleagues, the marketing directors and presidents of a range of youth and other museums that had recently gone through a tremendous expansion or opened a new facility. They gladly shared detailed data on their experiences and projections. We learned that we could expect attendance to double and that whatever bump we experienced likely would be followed by declines of 15 percent in each of the first two years before reaching a stabilized attendance level. And, in fact, while our initial year attendance tripled, the settling out was similar to what the others had predicted. How did I know who to call? Because the museum's leadership

Connie Duckworth

CONNIE IS THE youngest of the three girls in her family and has a brother ten years her junior. Her parents, Connie's biggest role models, stressed education and a strong work ethic, which has been instrumental in her success.

In 1976, Connie graduated Phi Beta Kappa from the University of Texas with a BA, and she received her MBA in finance and accounting from Wharton in 1979. She joined Goldman Sachs in 1981. In 1990, Goldman closed its Los Angeles office and Connie moved to Chicago to head the fixed income department. For a year, she commuted between Chicago and Los Angeles, where her husband stayed with their baby and his work. Despite help from Connie's in-laws, she and her husband decided that they'd prefer to have one at-home parent, so he left his job and the family moved to Chicago.

Connie's risky personal and professional move to Chicago paid off as she was promoted to partner at Goldman Sachs not long after. Currently, she is a managing director at Goldman Sachs and CEO of MuniGroup.com, an industry wide municipal bond marketplace formed by Goldman Sachs in partnership with other organizations.

Connie has received many awards, and serves on numerous boards, including Evanston Northwestern Healthcare Hospital, the Committee of 200, Wharton's Graduate Executive Board, the Trustee's Council of Penn Women, and the Visiting Committee of the University of Michigan. Connie and her husband have four children.

team regularly worked with its colleagues through both formal and informal networks, I simply reached out to existing contacts at the American Association of Museums, the Association of Youth Museums, and the Youth Museum Exhibit Collaborative, as well as at other local and national institutions.

"You need to be willing to stick your neck out and make the calls," notes Marilyn Lederer. When the museum needed to issue bonds, Lederer, who was then executive vice president of Chicago Children's Museum and had no background in that area, called on an old network and developed a new one to learn all about financing opportunities for the museum.

Helping others is an important aspect of building mutually beneficial relationships, and with Lederer's new knowledge she was able to assist several groups. She not only advised colleagues at other cultural institutions concerning their financing

DAWN Mello's networking took her around the world as she orchestrated the turnaround of Gucci, a global brand. The diverse team Mello assembled included Americans, British, and French, all of whom shared a common interest in reworking a once-great brand. She accomplished the turnaround, she notes, "through talking to people—gathering information and advice through others. You can't know it all; the jobs become too big for that. You need to work through others."

options, but also was able to put them in contact with the museum's underwriters, thereby helping both parties.

Susan Getzendanner uses her extensive network both to

Janet Robinson

JANET WAS BORN in 1950 and grew up in Massachusetts. She earned a BA in English from Salve Regina College in 1972.

Following graduation, Janet worked as a public school teacher and reading specialist for eleven years. In 1983, seeking a field in which performance is directly measured and rewarded, Janet joined the Times Company as an account executive at *Tennis* magazine. She was named advertising director of *Tennis* (1987), vice president of The New York Times Company women's magazine group (1990), and group senior vice president for advertising sales and marketing for that group (1992). Janet joined the *New York Times* newspaper in 1993 as a vice president, was named director of advertising (1994), senior vice president of advertising (1995), and president and general manager in 1996. Also in that year, Robinson completed the Executive Education Program at the Amos Tuck School at Dartmouth College.

Janet has received numerous awards, and was elected chairwoman of the board of directors of the American Advertising Federation for 1999. She serves on the boards of the Audit Bureau of Circulation, The Advertising Council, and the Fashion Institute of Technology as well as the presidential board of trustees of Salve Regina University. Janet also is a member of the Leadership Committee for the Lincoln Center Consolidated Corporate Fund. Janet is single and lives in New York City.

help others and to generate business. She comments, "The more people you know who think highly of you, the better off you are." For example, the only female board member at Waste Management was a Chicago Network member, as is Getzendanner. While that is not the reason that Getzendanner, partner at the law firm Skadden, Arps, Slate, Meagher & Flom, secured Waste Management's legal business, the fact that the board member knew and respected Getzendanner certainly didn't hurt.

Janet Robinson networks within and outside her industry to enhance her company's performance. Specifically, she learns best practices (techniques that work extremely well at other companies) that she can employ at the *New York Times* and also benchmarks her company's performance. Further, her service on the boards of the Advertising Council, the Fashion Institute of Technology, and the American Advertising Federation is not only good business but is personally fulfilling and part of her way to "give back."

Networking works, and women-to-women connections can be particularly helpful. Use them to your advantage.

While Janet Robinson uses networking as a tool to do her current job well, it also is a critical component of an effective job search. When Julia Stasch, then president of Shorebank, was appointed commissioner of Chicago's Department of Housing, she received approximately fifteen letters from female acquaintances with congratulations and staffing referrals of other women. Several of those introduced became part of her team. Networking works, and women-to-women connections can be particularly helpful. Use them to your advantage.

How Networking Within
Your Organization Helps You

While networking outside of your company and industry is important, you must not forget to develop a broad array of relationships within your organization. Internal relationships can help you move a project forward more quickly, receive choice assignments, be more visible, learn specific facts, find out how to navigate the waters at your place of employment, and have more fun. While you may, for short periods, minimize your time allocated to external networking, ignoring relationship-building activities within your own organization is a mistake. To be successful, you've got to build good relationships internally. Externally, it depends on where you are in your career.

No one can work in isolation. To accomplish objectives, you need allies throughout your company who trust you and will support your project. When Stephanie Shern assumed the role of vice chairman of industry services at Ernst & Young, she believed the firm needed to do more business with key players in targeted industries. In communications, for example, Ernst & Young was not working with the major telecommunications companies. To address this issue, Shern required support from across her company, including from area managing partners and those with a specific industry focus, to put together new teams and invest resources in developing new relationships and pieces of business. Shern concludes, "If one partner had to meet all the players for the first time, she'd still be working on it." Instead, because

To be successful, you've got to build good relationships internally.

Shern had already invested in relationships with her colleagues, the system could be put into place quickly and successfully.

On a more personal level, building your own visibility is an important aspect of networking and will serve you well within your own organization and beyond. As we saw in chapter six, Janet Gurwitch Bristow experienced the importance of visibility while working at Foley's department stores. Although she was rated the strongest performer in her group, another woman, more known to senior management, was promoted. When Gurwitch Bristow questioned the decision and developed relationships with those above her, she was soon promoted. From that experience forward, Gurwitch Bristow has worked to enhance her visibility as well as her skill.

I N terms of both building your visibility and understanding how your organization works, Lindy Hirschsohn, partner at The Boston Consulting Group, suggests, "Try to understand the key decision-making people and processes. It is like a neural network. You need to invest in the nodes." She delineates two buckets of people to cultivate: (1) people you like, and (2) people who will help you get where you want to go. Hirschsohn advises, "You need both buckets."

HOW CAN YOU BEGIN TO NETWORK?

Building networks is little more than creating a series of individual relationships, and you do it naturally every day.

Without even thinking about it, you are creating the basis for effective networks—in the halls at work, on airplanes or vacations, at sporting events or the gym. I, for example, met two authors who shared publishing tips with me through mutual friends at my children's school. Meaningful relationships can be formed anywhere.

While building relationships and networks may be second nature for some, a systematic approach works as well.

Try to invest a little time every day to build relationships with those around you.

Steps for creating a network include "doing what comes naturally," investing in relationships daily, joining and participating in relevant organizations, pursuing extracurricular interests, and being "out there."

Relationships need to spring from natural interests and expertise. You don't want your expertise to be networking unless you are a style (versus substance) person. While everyone needs role models and a professional network, it shouldn't be your end goal. Instead, develop relationships within your day-to-day circumstances—whatever they may be. Sharon Patrick, for example, met her current business partner, Martha Stewart Living Omnimedia CEO, Martha Stewart, climbing Mount Kilimanjaro in 1993. As they ascended, they traded business stories, and Patrick, an astute problem-solver, brainstormed with Stewart regarding issues Stewart faced. Thus, through the exchange of ideas, a relationship was established, and Stewart discovered an important ally to help her build her business, while Patrick secured an exciting client and ownership opportunity through her consulting business.

When you're pulled in lots of different directions, it's

hard to justify the extra effort to chat in the hall, and it's certainly hard to make time for an out-of-the-office lunch. But initiatives such as lunch, a round of golf, a sporting or cultural excursion, or even a joint manicure session do wonders for building camaraderie and establishing strong relationships. It's these smaller efforts along the way that make a difference, so try to invest a little time every day to build relationships with those around you.

Joining appropriate organizations is one way to meet people outside of your company and to learn from them. Whether you are starting out or more senior in your career, there is an association of people with similar jobs. Just attending a conference will provide you with information, and possibly contacts. And, as the old saying goes, the more you put into something, the more you'll get out of it. For example, Diane Swonk, senior vice president and chief economist for Bank One, puts a great deal of effort into her participation as a board member of the National Association of Business Economists. Over time, she has assumed a leadership role in the mostly male organization, and that provides her with an opportunity to meet people and refine her leadership skills outside of the office. Getting out gives you an opportunity to learn, and if you are not interested in learning, you'll limit your success.

Joining organizations that go beyond industry groups also can be helpful and interesting. United Way campaigns, for example, offer leadership opportunities where you can meet people from many different companies and industries while giving back to the community. Elynor Williams, president and managing director at Chestnut Pearson & Associates, got involved with the chamber of commerce in her

Diane Swonk

DIANE GREW UP in Ann Arbor, Michigan, as an only child. Since all her family's resources were focused entirely on her, Diane didn't experience the same limits other children did. Her parents divorced, but they remained close to her and gave her the skills she's used to become successful. Her mom, an art teacher, is creative and entrepreneurial. Her father, in contrast, has a business background and is mathematical and deliberate. He, like Diane, is dyslexic, and he demonstrated to Diane growing up that there are no such things as impediments—just different ways to do a job. In fact, her dad also has a speech impediment, and yet was known at General Motors for his speeches. Therefore, Diane didn't shy away from economics even though she flips numbers and finds writing difficult. Instead, she applies herself and has developed into a leading analyst, forecaster, writer, and speaker. Diane's passion for economics, the creative side of mathematics, blends the skills she inherited from both her parents.

The civil rights movement and other national and international phenomena in the 1970s also influenced Diane growing up. Her family encouraged an awareness of larger political and economic events and how they can have a local impact. Dinner table conversations were lively and would include discussions about China and Vietnam and how they affected the United States and Michigan. Seeing the local impact of the oil price shocks in the 1970s and of the huge increases in automobile imports from Japan sparked her keen interest in economics at an early age.

Diane earned her bachelor's and master's degrees in economics from the University of Michigan and her MBA from the University of Chicago. In 1985, Diane began her career at First Chicago Corporation, a predecessor to Bank One, as an associate economist. She rose through the ranks and was named deputy chief economist in 1995 and chief economist in 1999. Today, she is senior vice president and chief economist at Bank One.

Diane has been accorded many awards. She is a board member of the National Association of Business Economists and author of many of the bank's economic publications. She has released three nationally acclaimed studies, and her reports have been published by the Federal Reserve Bank of Chicago. Diane is called upon as an economic expert by policymakers from Chicago to Washington, and is one of the most quoted experts on the midwest economy. She is a regular commentator on CNN, a frequent guest on major news networks, and has appeared on *Wall Street Week* on PBS. While Diane wanted to be president when she was thirteen, today she aspires to be part of the Federal Reserve.

Diane is married and has two children.

hometown. She met a lot of people and that initiative led to a future job. Williams notes, "You need a broad base of people who know you. Don't tie your wagon to one star."

While Rose Marie Bravo does not participate in many group organizations, she suggests, "You need to do the right thing for your business. Especially at senior levels, but really at any level, it's part of your job and responsibility [to network as appropriate]." Networking was an important aspect of Bravo's life as president of Saks Fifth Avenue, and at I. Magnin before that. To represent the store, it was imperative that she "be part of the scene"—in touch with publishers, magazines, newspapers, and designers. Reflecting on these responsibilities, she advises, "Be out there."

Just how do you go about "being out there"? Valerie Salembier, publisher of *Esquire* magazine, notes, "It's hard to show up alone to an event, but take a deep breath and do it." Salembier recalls being invited to a cocktail dinner for a "women of distinction" group. She didn't know one person on the committee and didn't want to go. When she walked in, it seemed to her that everyone already knew everyone else. Her effort, however, paid off, as the person next to her at dinner became a close business and personal friend.

Salembier also remembers her first City Meals on Wheels lunch. She arrived thinking, "How many more women can I know?" The answer was several, since she ended up meeting women who became friends and business partners. Salembier believes, "There is always a wonderful surprise, whether in Oshkosh or Chicago or New York City."

Building relationships outside your organization isn't enough. As we saw with Janet Gurwitch Bristow and her delayed promotion at Foley's, you need to be visible internally too. Paula Sneed advises people (especially women, who are generally less inclined) to "put yourself in the light; be visible. Have the courage to step out of your comfort zone and connect with colleagues at a more senior level." That could involve signing up for projects outside the content of your day-to-day job or introducing yourself to the speakers and organizers at a gathering. Don't be afraid to approach others to make yourself known and to begin establishing a relationship.

Meaningful relationships can be formed anywhere. Your colleagues and those above and below you all end up someplace—and that someplace may be relevant to you over time. Robin Burns, president and CEO of Intimate Beauty Corporation and Victoria's Secret Beauty, and Andrea Jung, CEO of Avon, were both buyers at Bloomingdale's at the same time as Sue Kronick, chairman and CEO of Burdines. Now, while running three different companies, they can exchange ideas.

ONCE YOU'VE BUILT A RELATIONSHIP, WORK TO MAINTAIN IT

Don't take relationships for granted. From a pure efficiency standpoint, it takes more time, resources, and effort to build new relationships (or find new clients or customers) than to maintain existing ones. So don't forget to invest in relationships that you've already established by staying in touch, remembering small gestures, and going the extra mile for friends and colleagues. All will help you to maintain relationships.

You may be wondering, Just what kind of investment are we talking about? All little things. Take a moment to drop a note, make a call, or send an e-mail when you learn about a promotion or other event in someone's life. Or, let someone know that you are thinking of her, by sending a relevant newspaper article or Web site. If you've moved on to a new position or employer, let people know what you're doing and how they can reach you. The bottom line: Stay in touch. If you keep in contact with people, you won't feel awkward about picking up the phone to ask for something (such as information or a contact). You won't be connecting just when you need something because you will have been maintaining the relationship all along.

Try to stay in touch with all of your contacts. Indra Nooyi regularly calls friends at The Boston Consulting Group (BCG), Asea Brown Boveri, and Motorola, her previous employers, as well as clients from her BCG consulting days. Nooyi not only maintains contact but "goes the extra mile" for friends and colleagues. For example, a former BCG client asked Nooyi to recommend a contact at BCG and to review the proposal he received. She did both, and met with him on a Saturday morning to share her thoughts.

DON'T BURN BRIDGES

Another facet of building and maintaining relationships is taking care not to burn the proverbial bridge. You never know when and how other people may again play a role in your life. Don't just invest in maintaining relationships; be sure not to say or do things that preclude having an ongoing relationship with people. When Colleen Barrett's boss, Herb Kelleher, CEO and founder of Southwest Airlines, first formed the airline on paper, he spent three and a half years in court battling the big airlines that were trying to keep

Southwest out of the air. During this time, the president of Southwest became furious with Kelleher because Kelleher would joke with opposing counsel between sessions. While the president personalized what was happening and saw opposing counsel as an enemy, Kelleher developed relationships with them. Years later, when Southwest Airlines sought space at Detroit Metro Airport, Southwest employees told Barrett they tried everything and couldn't find anyone to lease them a gate—including Aviation Director Dick Jameson. Barrett said, "Is he a lawyer?" Sure enough, he formerly was part of American Airlines' legal team. As you'd guess, Kelleher subsequently called Jameson, who helped Southwest obtain new gates.

> M OLDING respectful relationships, even with people who appear not to be friends, is important in both good fortune and bad. Tanya Mandor notes, "The same people you meet on your way up are the first you'll meet on the way down. They can either help you or destroy you." Sheri Wilson-Gray echoes this sentiment, "It's important to get along with your peers. If they can't help you, they sure can hurt you."

Mentors

THE TERM "MENTOR" is a current buzzword and like the word "networking," it can be overused. The concept, however, is important. A mentor is someone from whom you learn in a participatory relationship. The mentor is actively engaged in guiding the protégé, often through feedback and example, and frequently tries to help the protégé advance in an endeavor. The protégé overtly tries to learn from the mentor and seeks that person for advice. While mentors are not essential to one's success, they certainly can be helpful.

How Mentors Can Help You

Mentors help you learn the ropes, expand your world, increase your visibility, learn from the negative as well as the positive, and distinguish yourself in a crowded field. Sometimes, too, you can move in lockstep with them up the ladder, and often they will play the role of sponsor, helping you to secure key promotions or assignments. Each of these aspects of a mentor/protégé relationship can help you work smarter, be more savvy, and navigate corporate waters more successfully.

Rose Marie Bravo had a number of role models and mentors, especially while she was a junior employee at Macy's. Through watching and working closely with mentors, Bravo was able to see how they solved problems and juggled competing demands. Rose Ann Cooper took Bravo under her wing and taught her about business and life at Macy's. For a while, Bravo moved up the ladder behind Cooper, who was ten years her senior and the consummate professional. When Bravo assumed positions recently vacated by her mentor, rather than feeling threatened, Cooper explained and expanded upon the strategies she had employed. And as Bravo worked for Cooper, their relationship, based on mutual respect, became a partnership. They were able to share issues and successes.

Bravo was an early mentor for Tanya Mandor, now

executive vice president at Revlon and another outstanding woman I interviewed. Earlier in her career at Macy's, Mandor returned from an international business trip, during which she missed her daughter's first birthday, and tried to resign, but Bravo helped her to find an opportunity, in cosmetics, that required less travel. Bravo's interest in Mandor and assistance with finding a better job fit taught Tanya what she considers rule number one: Help others. And, moving Mandor to cosmetics became a win-win—Mandor had a better fit, and Bravo retained a terrific employee.

Mentors also can help you increase your visibility.

Mentors can help you to see things more clearly within your world, and, importantly, they also can help you to expand your world. Michael Steinberg, as chairman of Foley's department stores, spent time exposing Janet Gurwitch Bristow to the forces that influence retail, including ballet and the arts. These lessons not only helped Gurwitch Bristow become a more successful retailer, but they also ignited her interest in joining the board of the Houston Symphony, where she developed new relationships. Additionally, Steinberg helped Gurwitch Bristow land her next job as executive vice president at Neiman Marcus.

Gurwitch Bristow's next two mentors were successive chairmen at Neiman Marcus: Terry Lundgren, now president of Federated Department Stores, and Burt Tansky, Neiman Marcus's current chairman. Each mentor taught her important business lessons, and today, their companies are significant customers of Gurwitch Bristow's relatively new cosmetics company. In fact, Neiman Marcus recently bought a 51 percent stake in Gurwitch Bristow's business.

Tanya Mandor

TANYA, WHO HAS an older sister and a younger brother, was born in Egypt in 1952 and lived in Africa and Europe before coming to the United States when she was twelve. Tanya's parents taught her that one's work ethic is as important as one's education, and that you should tackle problems with honesty and integrity and have a positive outlook on life.

Tanya graduated from Queens College with a BA in art and is a sculptor at heart. She began her career in Macy's executive training program in 1973 and worked there through 1988.

When Tanya, who is married to a devoted husband, had her first child at thirty-one, she planned to keep working. However, after missing her daughter's first birthday while in Hong Kong for Macy's, she decided to resign. Instead, her boss, Rose Marie Bravo found her a job in cosmetics that involved less travel. Then Tanya had a second child four years later, took a smaller job and later quit working altogether to spend more time with her family. Soon, she realized being a full-time mom was not the right fit for her, and when Revlon called about a marketing position, she jumped at the opportunity.

Mandor joined Revlon as director of marketing on the Ultima brand in 1989 and currently is executive vice president with global responsibility for all aspects of the Revlon brand.

Today her safety zone and reality check are still her close-knit family.

Thus, if you work to maintain the relationship, a mentor can help you achieve even after you no longer work at the same company. Ideally, the relationship, founded on mutual respect, transcends the job.

Mentors also can help you increase your visibility, as did Mary Ludgin's boss—first at JMB Realty Corporation and then at Heitman Capital Management. As a relatively junior employee at JMB, Ludgin proved to Charlie Wurtzebach through bold feedback and strong writing skills that she could be a trusted advisor. Subsequently, he began to feed her more responsibility and larger jobs. Wurtzebach also gave her valuable advice, invested company resources in Ludgin, and built her visibility by passing speaking engagements to her. When Wurtzebach became chief executive officer of Heitman, Mary became chief operating officer and, ultimately, succeeded him as CEO.

Frequently, there are many talented people in organizations, and especially in large institutions, it is easy

AS in anything, not all relationships are positive. Don't forget that you can learn as much or more from a negative experience. Looking for the lessons, in fact, can help you through those difficult spots. Tanya Mandor comments, "I learned more from the [managers] I didn't want to be like. For example, I had a manager who was fine with peers but terrible with subordinates. Another time, I experienced the humiliation you feel when reprimanded in front of others. I've worked for and been exposed to some real bears, but I wouldn't let them get the best of me."

to "get lost." Sheri Wilson-Gray notes, "You need to separate yourself one way or another to succeed, and relationships can make the difference. You need someone pulling for you. For example, at Procter & Gamble, where I used to work, there were many talented marketers. You needed to be on someone's lips to win." Having a sponsor or mentor can be the tiebreaker that secures the important assignment or promotion for you from among a crowded field of candidates.

How Do You Find a Mentor
and Build the Relationship?

Ideally, the mentor relationship develops naturally—through naturally occurring circumstances and based on mutual respect—but you can also be proactive and "help it happen." Be alert to the possibilities, and then work at developing mentor relationships when you see opportunities. If the relationships are not developing naturally, be proactive in seeking possibilities, but remember that both give and take are required, as they are in any successful relationship. Even if you are proactive, success is not guaranteed each time, as chemistry between two people is an important relationship component.

In terms of being aware of opportunities and working them appropriately, Nancy Karch, former director at the consulting firm McKinsey & Company, advises, "People should be conscious and seek mentors, though you can't make it happen. When it happens, it happens. But be aware of the importance of developing mentor relationships with senior people versus treating the relationships with senior folks as transactional." What Karch is saying is that when you have established a positive relationship with someone more senior through a work project, don't let the relationship die when the project ends. Rather, work to stay in touch. Then, instead of a one-time exchange, you have created an ongoing opportunity to learn and to share.

Once Karch realized the value of having a mentor—she came to believe it was essential to making partner—Karch employed an organized and systematic approach to learning from senior colleagues and finding reasons to spend time together. In short, she was proactive. When she encountered senior people she felt comfortable talking to, she made sure to do it regularly. She'd keep a list of questions and concepts that she was unsure of, and then she'd make an appointment to discuss them. When I employed this approach, I often looked for "down time" in my mentor's schedule, when she or he could take a breath and be more relaxed. That time may be early in the day or after the "crush" of business is done.

Although your mentor often will be senior to you, as with any relationship, give and take are essential. To be sustainable, the relationship must be mutually beneficial. Diane Swonk, who herself has mentored many people at Bank One, also has benefited from moving in lockstep with her boss and mentor.

The bottom line is to always be open to learning from others.

She notes, "To be really great in business, you need someone strong behind you to provide tail wind." Swonk's willingness to be the tail wind, she believes, has helped her to establish strong relationships as the protégé.

You cannot force a mentor-protégé relationship, since chemistry and mutual respect are two critical elements. As you work with a variety of people, some relationships will click,

Nancy Karch

NANCY, WHO HAS an older sister, grew up in a "terrific, stable, middle-class, suburban, Jewish family." Education and achievement were important, and both parents were supportive. They never made either child feel she had to justify her life choices. Nancy's sister, who earned an MS and an MBA, worked in banking but later devoted herself to being a full-time mom. Nancy, still unmarried, has pursued a rigorous professional career.

Nancy earned a BA in math from Cornell University in 1969, an MS in math from Northwestern University in 1971 and an MBA in 1974 from Harvard Business School, where she was a Baker Scholar. Nancy spent the next 26 years at McKinsey in the New York, Chicago and Atlanta offices. She rose to partner and then director and held several leadership positions, including managing partner of the retail practice and managing partner of McKinsey Southeast U.S.

In 2000, Nancy began a new phase of her professional life. She retired from McKinsey and now serves on the McKinsey Advisory Council, a small group of former directors who provide counsel to the firm. Additionally, Nancy has joined the board of directors of Liz Claiborne, and of Nabisco. She now resides in a small town outside of New York City.

based on the quality of your work and chemistry. A successful mentor-protégé relationship requires professional and personal sides: professional respect and personal liking.

Is There an Optimal Mentor?

There is no optimal mentor so build strong relationships where you can.

Inside Versus Outside Your Organization

It does not matter whether your mentor is inside or outside of your organization. The bottom line is to always be open to learning from others—whether they are in unusual or traditional positions, whether inside or outside your organization, or whether senior or junior to you.

Mentors at your own company are more likely due to day-to-day proximity and shared goals, and they can better help you advance within your company, However, external mentors may provide additional perspective. Robin Foote found mentors outside her place of employment, including her father and other males in his generation. Marilyn Lederer adds, "It's sometimes easier to have mentors outside your organization because they can be more objective." Lederer, for example, got career advice from Nancy Brandt, a former housewife who returned to work and became a senior executive at Bank of America.

Male Versus Female

It does not matter whether your mentor is male or female as long as two basic criteria are met: mutual respect and chemistry. The majority of the women I spoke with cited male mentors, but that is because males were most often the ones ahead of them on the career path. As more women make it up the ladder, women mentoring women will become more common.

A few women I interviewed did indicate that in predominantly male environments, women are not perfect advocates for other women. In that environment, when women sponsor other women (because there are so few), it is looked at more suspiciously. As the critical mass of females in positions of power grows, it will not be as unusual to have women naturally working together and developing relationships; therefore, when one woman sponsors another, it will not be considered "women just looking out for women."

Formal Versus Informal Mentor Programs

Many companies now have formal mentor programs. These programs provide benefits, although they don't work as well as naturally evolving relationships, since they are more of a job. Cynthia Round notes, "Formal programs don't work without real connections." Her experience comes from mentoring international students at Columbia University, which was similar to my experience with a Kellogg Women in Business program. I was available for discussions and meetings, but a day-to-day give-and-take working relationship never developed.

> *As more women make it up the ladder, women mentoring women will become more common.*

MENTORING OTHERS: YOUR RESPONSIBILITY

As you rise up in your place of employment, it is important to help others, especially those who have not traditionally had as many opportunities. That is an obligation recognized and welcomed by all of the women interviewed for this book. They were uniformly interested in the topic, generous with their time, insights, and experiences, and anxious to help other women progress more quickly. For only when women are sitting at the table will they be able to write the rules.

◆ POWER POINTER *Women-to-women connections work. As you go about gathering information, solving problems, or learning the ropes at your place of employment, do not undervalue your connections with other women. Your shared gender provides you with a commonality—a sisterhood of sorts—that can be powerful. Girlfriends you had growing up may be doing interesting things. Your sisters may be strong resources, and other women in your company or industry may be powerful aides over time. I secured the interviews used in this book through networking. I started with the outstanding women at places I used to work—Goldman Sachs, McKinsey & Company, and Chicago Children's Museum. And each female business leader I interviewed introduced me to several others at the pinnacle of the business world. To the extent that there ever was a time when women did not support other women, it is no longer the case. Women want to help other women rise through the ranks. Women-to-women connections work.*

CHAPTER SEVEN SUMMARY AT-A-GLANCE

Use the checklist below to make sure you understand the points and steps discussed in chapter seven.

NETWORKING

Networking can help you to
- ☑ Gather information and build your expertise.
- ☑ Generate business.
- ☑ Help others.
- ☑ Accomplish large objectives.
- ☑ Learn best practices; bench-mark performance; do your job well, and "give back."

Networking within your organization can help you to
- ☑ Develop broad support necessary to move projects forward.
- ☑ Build your visibility and momentum.
- ☑ Understand the decision-making process.

How can you begin to network?
- ☑ Do what comes naturally.
- ☑ Invest daily.
- ☑ Join relevant organizations and participate.
- ☑ Pursue "extracurricular" interests.
- ☑ Be out there.
- ☑ Take a deep breath and do it.
- ☑ Make yourself visible internally.
- ☑ Remember, meaningful relationships can be formed anywhere.

Once you've built a relationship, work to maintain it.
- ☑ Stay in touch.
- ☑ Take time for small gestures.
- ☑ Go the extra mile for friends and colleagues.

Don't burn bridges.
- ☑ Don't rule out having future relationships with people.
- ☑ If colleagues can't help you, they still may be able to hurt you.

MENTORS

Mentors can help you to
- ☑ Learn the ropes.
- ☑ Expand your world.
- ☑ Achieve, even if you no longer work at the same company.
- ☑ Increase your visibility.
- ☑ Distinguish yourself in a crowded field.
- ☑ Learn from the negative as well as the positive.

How do you find a mentor and build the relationship?
- ☑ Be alert to the possibilities.
- ☑ Be proactive.
- ☑ Recognize give and take are required.
- ☑ Remember, chemistry is integral to the relationship.

Is there an optimal mentor?
- ☑ They can be inside or outside your organization.
- ☑ They can be male or female.
- ☑ Formal mentor programs can help, although they are less effective than natural relationships.

Mentoring others is your responsibility.

If You Don't Ante, You Can't Win

🐟 POWER POINTER   *Trust your instincts.*

Y OU'VE GOT TO take risks, otherwise you will be immobilized," says Susan Getzendanner. There's no getting
around it. To move forward, you have to take risks. As
any card player can attest, if you don't ante, you can't play;
and if you're not playing, you sure can't win. The same is
true in business. The world is moving fast all around us, so
if you stand still, you'll get passed by. What worked yester-
day, and even what works today, may not be right for tomorrow. Therefore, change is not an option; it's an imperative.
And change is risky. But then again, doing nothing—not
innovating and not taking risks—is often the worst and most
risky strategy.

Risk-taking may not be comfortable for many of us, and
as you'll see, it's not even comfortable for many of today's
top business leaders. Given, though, that it's necessary, you
often must push yourself professionally and personally beyond
your comfort zone. How, then, can you be smart about risk?
There are two keys. First, take calculated risks. And second,

have contingency plans in place, including flexible resources so you can adapt to the situation as it unfolds. If you operate with these two simple principles in mind, you will be more comfortable and effective in the business world—and beyond, since the same risk-related principles hold, no matter what you do.

Push Yourself Beyond Your Comfort Zone

PUSHING YOURSELF is a facet of risk-taking and a key to success in the business world. If you wait until you feel completely comfortable trying something new, you may never do it. Even if you do eventually move forward, you may have waited too long. Instead, leaders frequently push themselves until it feels as though they "live on the edge." Even Julia Stasch—who has run a large private-sector business, served as number two in the U.S. General Services Administration, and now is Chicago mayor Richard Daley's chief of staff—occasionally harbors a deep secret fear that she'll be found out. She worries that people may discover that she doesn't have all the answers, or possibly the skills, to be where she is. For Stasch and other leaders, though, the fear of being immobilized is greater than the fear of being "found out." They realize that in order to move forward, you must put yourself on the line.

Don't worry about a small amount of anxiety as you take on a new assignment, make an important decision, or try something that you haven't previously done. It's only natural. And it will get your adrenaline flowing to help you operate at a higher level. Mary Ludgin frequently accepts speaking engagements on topics for which her boss, not she, is the expert. She has learned to research the audience and

Julia Stasch

J ULIA WAS RAISED in Illinois and has a younger sister. As Julia grew up, her parents' defining message to her was, "You can do anything." That message gave her confidence and empowered her to try many things.

Julia is a graduate of Loyola University and received an MA in American history from the University of Illinois at Chicago. For much of her career, Julia worked for Stein & Company, a Chicago-based real estate services firm. She started there in 1977, and in 1991, she was appointed president and chief operating officer. She then moved on to serve as president and CEO of Shorebank Chicago Companies, the nations first community development bank. In 1993, Stasch was chosen by President Clinton to serve in Washington, D.C., as deputy administrator of the U.S. General Services Administration, a twenty-thousand-person agency with an annual financial impact of $65 billion. In 1997, Stasch was appointed by Mayor Richard J. Daley as commissioner of the Chicago Department of Housing, and she became his chief of staff in 1999. Julia's accomplishments have been profiled in numerous national publications.

Julia is married and resides in Chicago.

the issues, be a quick study, take a point of view, and convey it captivatingly to those assembled. She moves beyond her own comfort zone in order to help her boss and build her own exposure and reputation.

You can learn to operate outside of your comfort zone by constantly pushing yourself to excel. Cynthia Round, the first in her family to attend college, had never traveled beyond her native Oklahoma when she interviewed and moved to Cin-

If you don't take risks and move forward, you'll never know what more you could have accomplished.

cinnati for a new job at Procter & Gamble. As we've seen, a few years later, her adventurous spirit propelled her to accept larger professional and cultural risks when she relocated to Italy to launch the Pampers brand there. She did not speak Italian and previously had not left the country. Her risk was rewarded, as she developed a new platform of skills and experience that propelled her to return to New York City and launch a successful career in advertising.

It's Better to Try and Fail Than to Fail to Try

There are many reasons why risk-taking is integral to success. First, if you don't take risks and move forward, you'll never know what more you could have accomplished. Second, if you don't take risks, someone else will, and they'll eat your lunch. The competition will take away your market share, for example, or decrease the value of what you are doing, since they have innovated and moved forward faster. Third, you won't be maximizing your knowledge base. There are important lessons that come from success and many more that arise from failure. Those lessons are both specific to the situation and more general, such as learning how to pick oneself up and move on.

Debi Coleman, chairman of Merix Corporation, notes, "I didn't learn as much from the easy successes as from failures and difficult situations." After Coleman graduated from Stanford Business School, she worked in finance at Hewlett-Packard, where she got involved in everything. There were no other MBAs, and Coleman thought she was the cat's meow—that is, until her boss two levels up sat her down and said, "You are driving us crazy. You have so many balls up in the air, you always propose new things, and you rarely finish anything. Not everyone agrees on your value to the organization because you are so disruptive." After hearing him through, Coleman went for a half-hour cry in the parking lot. And then she pulled herself together and got to work.

THE key to failure is to learn from it. Julie Bick recounts in her book *All I Need to Know in Business I Learned at Microsoft* that at Microsoft failure is examined, not punished. In fact, those who have tried something and failed frequently are promoted. The reason, Bick notes, is that the company doesn't want to lose all that great knowledge gained from the effort. This model, of course, assumes that you recognize and internalize the lessons from your failure, and that, therefore, you will be smarter the next time around. Making the same mistake twice is inexcusable.

In the next three months, Coleman organized and attacked her responsibilities and finished absolutely everything she had started. And then she received a major promotion. This difficult experience taught Coleman to see projects through to completion and that she could learn from feedback and use difficult situations to become stronger. Her "recovery" gave her confidence to overcome setbacks in the future and to keep going.

Take Calculated Risks

HOW DO YOU take risks and still set yourself up to succeed? Smart risk-taking involves taking calculated risks and building in contingency plans. Successful people are placing business "bets" every day. But they are making the odds work for them through fastidious research and informed judgment. As Janet Robinson, president of the *New York Times,* aptly notes, "If you surround yourself with the best people and data, the risks are calculated and become more marginal."

Robin Burns does her homework, and then, if she's confident, she bets big. After she left Bloomingdale's, where she oversaw the cosmetics division, Burns went to Calvin Klein Cosmetics Company to build that nascent business. There, under her leadership, the expenditure to launch Obsession perfume was more than twice the revenue of the entire company the previous year. How did Burns know to make such a large, seemingly risky outlay? The answer is, she didn't know, but she strongly suspected such a plan would lead to success. She based her decision on her own experiences and extensive research. At Bloomingdale's, she had launched many new fragrances, so she knew what was required for success in product development, marketing, and sales. Then,

Robin Burns

R OBIN, AN ONLY child, grew up in Colorado; her mother taught school and her stepfather was a mining and tunnel engineer. Robin worked summer jobs from the time she was thirteen. By her senior year at Syracuse University in 1974, Robin was still not sure what she wanted to do following graduation, so through on-campus interviews she talked to big companies that had training programs. Robin was most interested in retailing and most impressed with Bloomingdale's because she saw a clear career path for women.

During Robin's nine years at Bloomingdale's, she rose from the executive training program to merchandise manager of the cosmetics division. In 1983, Robin joined Calvin Klein Cosmetics Company as president and guided its phenomenal growth. In 1990, after several calls from Leonard Lauder, Robin joined Estee Lauder USA as president and CEO, and in 1995, her responsibilities were expanded to include Puerto Rico and Canada. In 1998, Robin was lured to The Limited to be president and CEO of a new subsidiary, Intimate Beauty Corporation, which will house a portfolio of new beauty companies including Victoria's Secret Beauty.

Robin serves on the boards of the Fashion Institute of Technology; the Cosmetics, Toiletry, and Fragrance Association; the Fragrance Foundation; S.C. Johnson Wax; and the Center for Gender Equality.

Robin is married and resides in New York.

at Calvin Klein, Burns studied other successful new products. She learned that if you think and act small, then you make a small impact. In contrast, the best way to break through the marketing clutter of competing products is to make a big investment—to think big and act accordingly. When Burns's intuition and the data matched, she moved forward aggressively. Burns's thorough research made the "calculated risk" manageable. In fact, she came to see her enormous expenditure not as a risk but as insurance for success.

Smart risk-taking involves taking calculated risks and building in contingency plans.

What are some of the lessons from Robin Burns's experience? First, don't let fear immobilize you. Second, decisiveness is critical. Once you've done your homework, be willing to make a decision and move forward to execute. A decision without effective execution is worthless. In the Obsession example, had Burns done her homework but been afraid to move forward decisively as the facts indicated, she might have selected a smaller budget and then failed to get her message through to consumers, thereby dooming her new brand to failure. Instead, Burns took a calculated risk and moved decisively to set up her company, her product, and herself for success. Therefore, the third lesson, as indicated above, is that sometimes you have to take sizable risks to win big.

At Revlon, Tanya Mandor was part of a team that believed strongly in a new lipstick technology that prevented lipstick from "kissing off"—coming off on people or napkins. While Revlon's laboratory had the technology for years, an internal faction, as well as the competition, thought the potential new products would fail. They believed that its benefits would be hard to communicate, and that its qualities were too different from those consumers were accustomed to. So why launch the product? Mandor and her team studied the market and recognized a "need gap." Women wanted, but did not have, a lipstick that stayed on. To counteract the perceived negatives, Mandor planned the communication strategy around them and was less aggressive in the initial launch. With their plans in place and the support of other risk-taking senior managers, they pushed forward and changed the business by bringing technology into it. Today, ColorStay lipsticks accounts for a significant component of Revlon's product line.

WHEN Sue Kronick ran textiles at Bloomingdale's, she made the seemingly risky decision to drop a successful multimillion-dollar business. Specifically, she got out of 180 thread-count poly-cotton bed sheets, the backbone of the business. Instead, Kronick switched to higher quality all-cotton products because Wal-Mart was moving into Bloomingdale's former territory. Kronick concludes, "If you don't place big bets, it's hard to win. Certainly, you can't win big, and you likely won't win at all because someone around you is betting."

Develop Contingency Plans

ONE OF THE most effective tools for maximizing your returns while minimizing your risk in any new situation is contingency planning. Contingency planning enables you to manage your risk by preparing for a range of possible outcomes of a particular scenario. Don't let yourself be surprised. Instead, anticipate. Situations never play out precisely as you plan, so plan for that. Have available extra and flexible resources above and beyond those you believe necessary for the desired (and, ostensibly, most likely) outcome. Chart what you'll do and how you'll accomplish it if your plan is fully, partially, or not at all successful.

Don't let yourself be surprised. Instead, anticipate.

The exercise itself of planning for a range of outcomes may help you to strengthen your primary or A plan by forcing you to consider a broad spectrum of possibilities. And by developing B, C, and D plans, you will be ready for almost any situation that unfolds.

Betsy Holden used contingency planning when she rolled out DiGiorno pizza with minimal testing—when others said it couldn't be done. Holden's team had cutting-edge technology for self-rising pizza and wanted to bring its new product to market in record time, since winter is a big pizza season. In order to meet its aggressive objectives without all the usual tests, the team examined every part of the process and what could go wrong. Then they crafted their plans. For every aspect of the launch, they made sure they had flexible resources available.

- **Production:** They sent a team member to Germany to study the equipment and how to handle breakdowns.

- **Packaging:** As they were using unique packaging that hadn't previously been put to the test, they accessed packaging experts within Kraft who could help with backups if they were needed.
- **Sales:** The sales force developed sales contingencies, so that if timing of the product launch slipped, they had a plan for how to delay or adjust the strategy.
- **Marketing:** Various scenarios were developed, such as: If we don't get x-percent consumer trial and y-percent repeat purchase, then we'll do these three things. If we exceed x and y, we'll do these three other things.

The key is that Holden's team did not wait to see how the process unfolded before developing alternative (B, C, and D) plans. So, regarding marketing, they knew how they would handle deviations if sales were short or if they exceeded expectations. Holden notes, "That's how you de-risk things that people are afraid to do."

Situations never play out precisely as you plan, so plan for that.

In our fast-changing environment, you may spend a great deal of time in places others haven't been. There is no "history" to look back on, and key assumptions frequently change. Therefore, consider three things for each step of your process: (1) What could go wrong?; (2) How can I improve the plan?; and (3) How will I respond to the alternate possible scenarios? Then you, like Holden, can move forward into new territory confidently and successfully.

Take Personal Risks

THE EXAMPLES ABOVE explore risks taken as part of a business. However, to maximize your own success, you also must take risks with your career. These personal risks often include taking risks with your career path, staking out an unpopular position, and standing up for principles. In each instance, confidence in yourself and the courage of your convictions will help you to forge ahead.

Career path risk can entail accepting a promotion or new assignment before you are certain you are ready, moving to a new location, or changing jobs. Carole Black had no network television station experience when she accepted a position as president of KNBC Television in Los Angeles. Her lack of experience represented a risk for both NBC and Black. However, as she and her boss anticipated, her skills were transferable, and under Black's leadership, KNBC soared to become the dominant number-one television station in its market.

When Dianne Sautter took a job as head of Chicago Children's Museum in 1983, there were a lot of great cultural institutions in Chicago and little public support for the new children's museum project. It was not a sure bet that the concept would succeed. It took fifteen years and three moves for the museum to reach its permanent home. Under Sautter's leadership, the museum grew from a hallway in the Cultural Center to an institution that serves more than five hundred thousand people annually and is the city's fifth-most visited cultural institution and the nation's second-most visited youth museum. If Sautter had been afraid of failing, the community would not have had the benefit of her passionate leadership.

Dianne L. Sautter

DIANNE GREW UP in a military family and consequently moved from base to base. That constant movement enabled her to see lots of new things and made her comfortable with change. She was strongly influenced by her father, who enjoyed exploring and adventure.

Dianne received a degree in special education and elementary education from the University of Illinois at Champaign-Urbana. She taught in the Chicago public schools for five years, helped open Chicago's first magnet school program, and directed a parent/teacher resource center before joining Chicago Children's Museum in 1983 as the founding executive director and president. She was the first full-time staff member, and her vision and leadership have guided the museum's growth to become the second-most visited youth museum nationally.

Dianne's leadership includes involvement with several national and local organizations devoted to children's activities and welfare. She is a governing council member of the Association of Youth Museums, serves on the executive board of the Urban Libraries Council, and is a peer reviewer for the Institute of Museum and Library Services. Dianne was a 1997 national delegate to the president's Summit for America's Future and is involved in a leadership capacity in a number of local Chicago organizations as well.

Dianne is married, has one stepson, and resides in Illinois.

Today's fast-paced world of mergers and acquisitions produces both opportunity and peril for many employees. As we saw in chapter two, when accounting companies Ernst & Whinney and Arthur Young merged, Stephanie Shern was a partner in the retail group at Arthur Young. Following the merger, she identified two potential paths for herself: she could stay in her practice group and watch developments unfold, or she could throw herself into the new firm and new opportunities. Shern chose the latter, thereby giving up the comfort of her existing situation and risking working with and for all new people. It turned out to be the best thing she could have done for herself. That calculated risk enabled her to get where she is today—on the management committee and vice chairman of the combined entity.

Marilyn Lederer took

BARBARA Scholley's upbringing taught her that there was nothing she couldn't do if she worked at it, and motivates her to employ a "Why shouldn't I try that? What do I have to lose?" approach to her career in the U.S. Navy. Although the navy's dive program required better physical conditioning than many other opportunities and had far fewer women, she decided to give it a try. Following her success in that program, Scholley has worked to highlight for women the less traditional paths open to them in the navy. Scholley's willingness to take risks, to push herself, and to try new things are just a few of the many reasons that she became the fourth woman ever to take command of a navy ship.

personal risk to switch careers while raising three young children alone. "Reentering the workforce in a whole new field was scary, especially as a single parent raising three young children," comments Lederer. Following her 1985 divorce, Lederer needed to support her family, provide a positive role model for her children, and find the intellectual stimulation she craved.

As Lederer pondered her future, she realized, with some trepidation, that what she had devoted her educational career to—preparing to teach college French—was not how she wanted to spend her life. Consequently, Lederer talked to friends who were returning to work following time off for families. One, who had been a junior high school teacher, was taking accounting classes. Accounting also appealed to Lederer, who, as an undergraduate at the University of Michigan, had considered pursuing her MBA, but with few women treading that path, had not taken the risk. Ironically, Lederer, saddled with many additional responsibilities, now decided to charge ahead. She began an entry-level bookkeeping job and started taking courses, and soon realized that she not only liked accounting but was good at it. Thus, over the next seven years, Lederer took the personal and professional risks required to complete the necessary classes to sit for the certified public accountant (CPA) exam, all while working full-time and raising her children.

A number of times Lederer considered giving up on her quest to become a CPA. She studied evenings after she finished up at the office and helped her children with their homework, and was frequently exhausted. Therefore, she was particularly discouraged in 1989 when she passed just half of the CPA exam. During such challenging times, Lederer "dug deep" and drew inspiration from her father, who had been an important role model and mentor. She explains, "As my grandfather was killed when my father was just seven, he became enterprising young, selling newspapers at eight and later working at a soda fountain. With little formal education, at eighteen, he started as a shipping clerk in a privately held trucking company and ultimately rose to become chairman of the board." As Lederer grew up, she watched how her father handled the many challenges he encountered. By example and through explicit teaching, he conveyed to his daughter that, "The world is yours to take. You have lots of opportunities."

In 1991, overcome by emotion, Lederer cried at the mailbox as she retrieved the affirmative results of her second CPA exam. Her mix of feelings included relief and pride: relief and pride that she, indeed, had climbed the mountain and achieved her personal goal of becoming a CPA. And pride that she had shown her children that taking risks and pursuing your dreams is important, and that what you set out to do the first time in your life isn't always where you end up. She proved to them and to herself that if you take personal risks, you can change and be successful in different directions. You can follow your dreams, wherever they may lead.

> *In an environment composed of people who act with integrity, standing up for your principles ultimately engenders respect.*

Taking an unpopular position is another type of personal risk you will encounter in the business world. When Lederer worked as executive vice president at Chicago Children's Museum, she noticed that a senior staff member who reported to the president was not making it, and although it was not advice the president wanted to hear, she sounded

Marilyn A. Lederer

M ARILYN, WHO HAS an older sister, has been influenced by her father throughout her life. He communicated a positive, can-do attitude, whether Marilyn was learning to skate, tackling a difficult subject at school, or considering career issues. He conveyed through word and deed—such as when he took up competitive tennis at age fifty and learned computers in his seventies—that there are no limits if you believe in yourself. He also instilled in Marilyn a selfless generosity that is part of what led her to pursue her career in the nonprofit field.

Marilyn earned a bachelor's degree in French from the University of Michigan in 1970, and after college she got married and had three children, following the example of her mother, a full-time homemaker. When Marilyn and her husband divorced in 1985, Marilyn re-entered the workforce to support her family as a single mom. Marilyn's three children have been a guiding force and primary motivator in her life.

Marilyn became a certified public accountant in 1991, and from 1986 to 1993, she served as executive director of National Lekotek Center, a nationwide network of toy-lending libraries for children with disabilities and their families. From 1993 to 1998, Marilyn was executive vice president of Chicago Children's Museum, and in 1998, she became chief operating officer of The CHEST Foundation. Marilyn is a member of numerous professional organizations and serves on the board of directors of the Happiness Club.

the alarm. For a while, Lederer's relationship with the president was uncomfortable; however, Lederer's courage to speak up based on her convictions helped to strengthen the institution for which she worked.

Standing up for principles can be risky in the short term, yet it is of critical importance to your long-term success. In an environment composed of people who act with integrity, standing up for your principles ultimately engenders respect. Mary Ludgin experienced this phenomenon in her first days working at Heitman Capital Management. Following the acquisition by Heitman of JMB Institutional Realty, where Mary worked, a senior executive at Heitman yelled at Ludgin. When he approached Ludgin, he was already angry and hadn't even bothered to read Ludgin's background document on the topic at hand. Offended by his approach, Ludgin told him that if he didn't want to review her material and preferred to yell rather than to discuss, then he could please leave her office. While Ludgin worried about the consequences of her statement, she felt she could only operate in an environment of mutual respect. In the end, though the person did not become a close friend, he now respects Ludgin.

See Opportunity Where Others See Only Risk

WITH POSITIVE AND perceptive thinking, you can spot opportunity where others see peril. When Jane Thompson took over Sears' Home Services, she was charged with creating a new business model from a business that essentially lay dormant. Given this objective, she invested hundreds of millions of dollars and undertook a major business redesign. While some would have been paralyzed by the perceived risk, Thompson spied an opportunity to improve the business.

An area often filled with opportunity, particularly for women, yet perceived as risky, is a turnaround situation. Why do I say that turnarounds represent strong opportunities for women? Because in periods of rapid change, growth, or upheaval, established norms are thrown out the window and nontraditional solutions are sought. That translates into greater opportunities for women managers—who are still less likely to be picked for leadership positions in corporate America. Your chances of rapid advancement and leadership roles are greatest in industries (such as the Internet), companies, and divisions undergoing rapid growth, change, or trauma.

Also, the perceived risk in turnaround situations is often overstated. If the situation is a mess before you arrive, your risk is mitigated. If you succeed in improving the business, then you are a hero. And if you are unable to improve the situation, well, it was a mess when you arrived.

A third and equally salient point is that in a turnaround situation there is a lot to learn. By definition, the working environment must change quickly, and therefore you will learn fast. You will learn both from the mess that was created and also from the trajectory or path of recovery. These lessons of how to right a bad situation are powerful, valuable, and transferable. That's why, during the early 1990's recession, "turnaround specialists" were among the most highly paid business professionals in the world. The best among them moved, after relatively brief stints, from company to company, making millions of dollars with options packages tied to the recovering stock price. Whether you are leading the turnaround charge or are part of the team, your experience will be highly valuable to you and any future employer.

How can you create value for yourself from turnaround situations? Seek them out, work smart, and communicate your success when it occurs. For marketers, that might entail seeking to work on a brand that is in trouble. Irene Rosenfeld made a name for herself as a young marketer after taking the helm of Kraft's struggling beverage group. By creating

Your chances of rapid advancement and leadership roles are greatest in industries, companies, and divisions undergoing rapid growth, change, or trauma.

savvy ads for children and making the Kool-Aid product less sweet for moms, the business began growing for the first time in years. Later, she revived Jell-O, and today she oversees the strengthening of Kraft's Canadian business as its president.

In 1992, Gail McGovern was put in charge of AT&T's toll-free 800-number business just as customers were given portability—meaning they could switch to lower cost carriers but keep their 800-number. AT&T was expecting to lose 10 percent market share, so on the surface, the job seemed like a no-win, risky proposition. Instead, through smart customer understanding and savvy marketing, McGovern boosted customer service and emphasized AT&T's reliability. When the dust settled, AT&T lost just 2 percent market share, and within three years McGovern was an executive vice president running the business-service operations.

Carly Fiorina's ability to spot opportunity where others see risk has provided her with outstanding business experience. She related the following story in a first-person article in the *New York Times* on September 29, 1999, titled "Making the Best of a Mess": "It was 1984, I was thirty years old and working at AT&T. The company's divestiture had just occurred, the Bell operating companies had just been spun off, and things were in shambles. Access Management, the division responsible for connecting long-distance calls to local phone companies, was in the worst shape. I decided that's where I wanted to work.

"People thought I was nuts," Fiorina noted. "Nobody knows what they're doing, people said. It's a mess. And that's exactly what appealed to me. It was a wonderful challenge. I knew I could have a big impact, for better or for worse."

Though Fiorina knew nothing about the Access Management division, she learned all she could from two excellent engineers on her team. They discovered that AT&T's biggest single cost was from bills from local companies, and that AT&T had no way of knowing if those bills were correct.

"This is not something that most people would think of as fun. Nevertheless, our goal became to verify every bill and prove every overcharge. We decided we must create a billing verification system. Eventually, this system was implemented all over the country by hundreds of employees and saved the company millions of dollars. We had great fun accomplishing something nobody thought we could."

Fiorina's turnaround experience proved her capabilities to her colleagues and superiors at AT&T and helped her to progress quickly up the ladder there and later at Lucent, when that group was spun off from AT&T. In September 1999, in a move heralded on the cover of many business magazines, Fiorina was tapped to run Hewlett-Packard and "turn around" its position in the fast-changing Internet environment.

As you push yourself to take risks, keep in mind this sage piece of advice that a mentor once shared with Elynor Williams: "Reach for the stars, and if you fall, you may find yourself among the clouds." The point is, push yourself to excel, and even if you fail at a particular endeavor, you will still be someplace terrific for having tried.

➤ POWER POINTER *Trust your instincts. Although there are many common sayings regarding the power of a woman's intuition, the surprising truth is that in the business world, men trust and rely on their instincts more than women do. There is power, however, in trusting your instincts and moving boldly when your instincts and the facts line up. Otherwise, as Phyllis Apelbaum's mentor, Dr. Jessie Potter, said, "When you always do what you always do, you'll always get what you always got. What will you do to make a difference?"*

CHAPTER EIGHT SUMMARY AT-A-GLANCE

Use the checklist below to make sure you understand the points and steps discussed in chapter eight.

Push yourself beyond your comfort zone.
- ☑ Learn to work past the anxiety that accompanies risk.
- ☑ Recognize that it's better to try and fail than to fail to try.

Take calculated risks.
- ☑ Do your homework.
- ☑ Prevent caution from getting in the way of good decisions.
- ☑ Act decisively.
- ☑ Have a flexible plan in place.

Develop contingency plans.
- ☑ Prepare for a range of possible outcomes.
- ☑ Have extra and flexible resources in place.

Take personal risks.
- ☑ Take career path risks.
- ☑ Risk taking an unpopular position.
- ☑ Stand up for your principles.

See opportunity where others see risk.
- ☑ Recognize that turnarounds provide opportunity.
- ☑ Realize rapid change and fast growth also provide opportunity.

To Thine Own Self Be True

☙ POWER POINTER *Use an honest assessment of your own strengths and weaknesses to your advantage.*

I N   M Y   I N T E R V I E W S, when I asked, "What advice do you have for others striving to be successful," the answers were heartfelt and clear. As you will see, they can be grouped into corollaries around the theme "to thine own self be true." Specifically, women at the helm of corporate America emphasize how important it is to know yourself, be yourself, have confidence in yourself, and act with integrity.

Know Yourself

THE FIRST STEP in knowing yourself is honesty. Begin with your overall values and life, and then move toward more specific attributes related to a job and career. What is important to you? What do you truly like and dislike? What are your strengths and weaknesses? Where do you want to go? Be careful not to confuse your own personality and goals with what others—whether parents, spouse, children, or friends—want for you. And make sure you focus on what

B E true to yourself. Know within your own value order what is success. Do you need institutional, financial, or progeny success? If you know that, it is easier to develop skills, prioritize, and focus. Figure out what is important to you and live to that. Know your values and reexamine them to make sure you are true to them," counsels Suzanne Nora Johnson, managing director at Goldman Sachs.

you really want, not on what you think you ought to want.

The well-known "eulogy exercise" may help you to determine what you'd like the core components of your life to be. As a reminder, if you were drafting your own eulogy, what would you want to be able to say about yourself? What would you want your family, friends, and colleagues to say? Now, what do you have to do to get to that point? Where do work, family, friends, community, and other interests fit into the equation, and how do you make them consistent with your values?

Linda Ellis wrote a poem, "The Dash," that eloquently presents these same ideas. It first showed up on the Internet from an anonymous source and later was identified as her work. I share it with you below.

"THE DASH" by Linda Ellis

I read of a Reverend who stood to speak
At the funeral of his friend.
He referred to the dates on her tombstone
From the beginning . . . to the end.
He noted that first came the date of her birth
And spoke of the following date with tears,

But he said what mattered most of all
Was the dash between those years.

For that dash represents all the time
That she spent alive on earth....
And now only those who loved her
Know what that little line is worth.
For it matters not, how much we own;
The cars ... the house ... the cash.
What matters is how we live and love
And how we spend our dash.

So think about this long and hard ...
Are there things you'd like to change?
For you never know how much time is left
(You could be at "dash mid-range").
If we could just slow down enough
To consider what's true and real,
And always try to understand
The way other people feel.

And be less quick to anger,
And show appreciation more,
And love the people in our lives
Like we've never loved before.
If we treat each other with respect,
And more often wear a smile ...
Remembering that this special dash
Might only last a little while.

So, when your Eulogy is being read
With your life's actions to rehash ...
Would you be proud of the things they say
About how you spent your dash?

—© 1998 Linda Ellis, www.lindaslyrics.com

ASSESS YOUR SKILL SET

Being realistic about your interests and capabilities within your specific job also will help you to succeed. Recognize your strengths and continue to develop them while acquiring select new ones. "Some people try to be everything. You can be broad, but always focus on doing one or two things exceptionally well," notes Janet Robinson. Knowing that Robinson's strong suits are sales and managing people helps her to succeed as president of the *New York Times*.

Recognize your strengths and nurture them.

If you have trouble analyzing just what your strengths and weaknesses are, seek feedback from others. Ask your colleagues, family, and friends for their thoughts. And don't be afraid to enlist professional help. That could be as simple as picking up a copy of *What Color Is Your Parachute?*, by Richard Nelson Bolles, the guide to self-assessment that has sold millions of copies and is now in its twenty-sixth printing or checking out careerdiscovery.com. Or it could involve completing the Myers-Briggs analysis, or hiring a professional counselor to guide you.

Your school placement office can help you locate the proper resources. If you attended a liberal arts program as an undergraduate and you are seeking a business-related job or advisor, you may want to try the affiliated graduate business school if there is one.

Sara, a friend of mine, located a fabulous career counselor through Kellogg Graduate School of Management at Northwestern University. As a single woman living in New York City, she had risen through the ranks to become a group magazine publisher. Later, in Chicago, working part-time as an investment banker and juggling the parenting responsibilities of her seven-year-old daughter, Sara felt isolated from New York and the hubbub of her fast-track career there. Not sure how to move forward professionally, Sara, who has a masters in management from Kellogg, contacted its placement office, which then put her in touch with a consultant who specializes in counseling accomplished businesspeople.

That consultant helps people identify and pursue their professional dreams. In order to help you pinpoint what you love and have talent for, he explores four areas: (1) your childhood; (2) your work experience and career development—to understand why you are successful at certain things; (3) your relationships with people; and (4) your management style.

While Sara pursued career-counseling services through her graduate business school, you may want to begin by exploring the resources and opportunities

WHEN Lindy Hirschsohn was having trouble contextualizing a piece of feedback, she sought additional resources. She asked her supervisor for a week to do some psychological tests, including Myers-Briggs, and to get some coaching. Although Hirschsohn offered to pay for the counseling, her firm was delighted by her interest in her own development and gladly supported her efforts. Hirschsohn believes that her initiation of the process coupled with her enhanced self-knowledge from the exercises helped her to be more effective and, ultimately, to make partner at The Boston Consulting Group.

Indra Nooyi

INDRA GREW UP in India in a family in which only one thing mattered: academics. Indra's mom, a remarkable woman, had wanted to "be something big," but her parents married her off before college. She was determined that her kids should go to college and do what they wanted in the world. In order to foster their development, she held monthly competitions for the children, in which they each would give a speech and compete for her vote. This exercise helped Indra develop confidence and a strong public speaking ability.

Indra earned a BS degree from Madras Christian College and an MBA from the Indian Institute of Management in Calcutta. After business school, she went to work for Johnson & Johnson in India and launched Stayfree. Then, at the behest of her friends in the United States, Indra moved to America and entered the Yale Public Management program.

After graduating from Yale, Indra worked for The Boston Consulting Group, Motorola, and Asea Brown Boveri. In 1994, she joined PepsiCo as senior vice president of corporate strategy and development and she added CFO responsibilities in 2000. She serves on the board of directors for Phoenix Home Life Mutual Insurance Company, Timberland, and the PepsiCo Foundation, and she is a member of the board of trustees for Convent of the Sacred Heart School in Greenwich, Connecticut. She and her husband have two daughters and a tight-knit nuclear and extended family.

available through your own employer. At Bank One, for example, there are human resources specialists available within the company who are charged with finding the right match internally between employees and job opportunities. Certainly, companies prefer working with strong performers in whatever capacity rather than losing them altogether.

Be Yourself

BEING YOURSELF IN a work environment is practical and important, as it is neither effective nor sustainable to try to be someone you are not. Of course, it helps to find a work environment in which you are comfortable and which values people such as yourself. Indra Nooyi challenges colleagues to accept her for who she is—a woman, mother, wife, and Indian professional. Her office is covered with pictures of her children. She routinely dresses in Indian-style clothing. And where her family is concerned, she does not hesitate to show emotion. When her daughter had Lyme disease, she shared her anxiety with her colleagues. But she is also professional and tough when it comes to work-related matters. Overall, Nooyi is comfortable with herself, lets others get to know her, and won't change to be someone she is not.

Being yourself enables you to take advantage of your own unique and positive qualities.

Being yourself also enables you to take advantage of your own unique and positive qualities. A colleague told Mary Ann Domuracki, when she worked at Ernst & Young, "Your smile and friendly manner are great assets in business. People feel comfortable around you and talk more, so you learn more." These assets suited her well when she worked for a time in Japan, as her Japanese clients found her quiet nature nonthreatening and sought her out for business.

Even in an environment as male-dominated as the armed services, a woman must be herself to succeed. Some of the most important advice Commander Barbara Scholley received was, "Don't try to change yourself to fit some mold that you think you should be." That counsel, received many times, gave Scholley confidence that she was succeeding in her own right. In contrast, Scholley observed some women who did change and lost most traces of their femininity. Over time, that strategy failed. Scholley notes, "We women are not the same as men. We must strive for equality of opportunity and experience—not sameness."

It is a common inclination to emulate those in power—and in a male-dominated work environment, that often is men. A better strategy, however, is to cherry-pick those attributes that you admire and that feel comfortable. Brenda Barnes recalls looking at different kinds of bosses, particularly one she had at the time and didn't respect, and wondering if she'd have to change to be like him to be successful. Upon reflection, she decided, instead, to be herself and not compromise her values. Her quick ascent through the ranks at PepsiCo to president and CEO of Pepsi-Cola North America by age forty-three is testimony to the wisdom of her decision to be herself. She summarizes, "It's too hard worrying about 'who I am' to get the job done."

You need to be comfortable with yourself and the choices you make because, invariably, there will be people who voice disapproval of your path. When Barnes was living apart from her husband and children during one period, people would criticize her as a mom and wife. However, she was satisfied with the choices she was making for her family and her career.

While it is important to be yourself, realize that there is a narrower band of acceptable behavior for women than for men in the business world. This "narrower band" is outlined by Anne Morrison of the Center for Creative Leadership in her book *Breaking the Glass Ceiling* and is adapted below. It refers to the fact that the business world is more accepting of and accustomed to typical male behavior. That is the norm and standard to which all are held. "Typical" female behavior is by and large not acceptable, and the common segment—or narrow band—where female behavior and acceptable (masculine) business style intersect is relatively small.

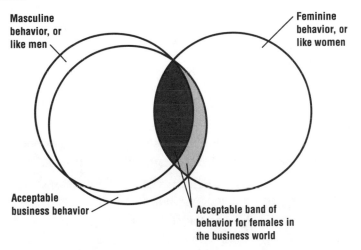

Masculine behavior, or like men

Feminine behavior, or like women

Acceptable business behavior

Acceptable band of behavior for females in the business world

Why, then, is it not advisable for women to act like men? First, as discussed above, it is not sustainable if it is not who you are. Second, and equally important, it is not acceptable. It does not fall in the accepted band of business behavior for

Brenda Barnes

BRENDA GREW UP in Chicago as the third of seven girls. She notes, "In terms of influence and impact, my parents are at the top of the list. They instilled in me a strong work ethic." Brenda's dad was a factory worker, and her mom stayed at home, except when they needed additional financial help.

Brenda graduated from Augustina College in 1975 in the midst of a recession. As she didn't have money for graduate school, she took a series of jobs, including becoming a waitress, an associate in a clothing store, and then a night shift mail sorter for the post office. Brenda, deciding that she hadn't gone to college for these sorts of jobs, quit and began knocking on doors. In 1976, a door opened at Wilson Sporting Goods. She started in distribution, viewing it as an interim job before returning to graduate school, but after a year, she moved to marketing and attended Loyola Business School at night. After five and a half years at Wilson, Brenda had become a product manager, but she believed she couldn't progress further and decided to quit. Her boss said, "Why go elsewhere for more consumer goods experience, when Pepsi-Cola and Frito-Lay are possibilities within the Pepsi company?" After receiving offers from both companies, Brenda moved to Dallas as senior product manager for Frito-Lay. She became vice president of marketing after three years.

A twenty-two-year Pepsi veteran, Brenda rose through

the ranks and was named president and chief executive officer of Pepsi-Cola North America in April 1996. She gave up her position in 1997 at the age of forty-three to spend more time with her family and participate in the business world through board work. She now serves as a director of The New York Times Company, Sears Roebuck & Company, Avon Products, Inc., Lucas Digital, and Starwood Hotels & Resorts. She noted at the time of her announced departure, which made front-page news around the world, "I hope people can look at my decision not as 'women can't do it' but as 'for twenty-two years Brenda gave her all and did a lot of great things.'" Retirement, however, was fleeting because, as this book went to press, Brenda had been called upon to serve as interim president and chief operating officer of Starwood.

Brenda is married and the mother of three children. Her husband, who has worked at McKinsey, General Electric, May Department Stores, and Pepsi, shares parenting responsibilities. In fact, they had a commuter marriage for eight years, and while Brenda was in Dallas, her husband was in Kansas with the kids.

women to exhibit or mimic male attributes and "malelike" behavior.

How does the narrower band of behavior manifest itself? Women must walk a much finer line, for example, between being assertive and being perceived as overly aggressive. Or, when presenting an idea, between being enthusiastic and being perceived as emotional. The narrower band of acceptable behavior is one of the central reasons why it's more difficult for women than men to succeed in a traditional business environment. You have to be bold, but not too bold; strong, but not strident. Today, the key is to expand the band through efforts by women, men, and corporate management.

Have Confidence in Yourself

A BELIEF IN yourself, or inner confidence, will make "being yourself" the natural choice. It also makes the climb up the ladder seem considerably less steep. Confidence is an ingredient in the recipe for success. Confidence enables you to (1) be yourself, (2) trust your instincts, (3) have the conviction to hold firm to your principles, and (4) communicate with assurance your views and hypotheses. Confidence also mitigates the destructive self-doubt regarding your actions that can eat you up and render you ineffective.

Today's leaders typically were raised with high expectations, and those expectations translated into confidence and a drive to succeed.

Susan Getzendanner's confidence has enabled her to become one of Chicago's top trial lawyers and a respected federal judge. She developed her self-confidence in high school as a successful debater. Getzendanner's awards for both debate and public speaking propelled her to enter professional situations thinking, "I can win this case." And it provided her with what she terms "the nerve necessary to be a judge and to rule as all quietly await your verdict."

Can self-confidence in a professional environment be developed? Absolutely. When Julia Stasch began at Stein & Company, she had little professional experience. Her ascent to president and CEO, however, was aided by Rich Stein, who believed in her and conveyed the idea, "You can do anything you want to; just try." He gave her a "blank slate" to exercise her ambition at the entrepreneurial company at an early stage of its growth. This experience as an adult made Stasch a more comfortable risk-taker by giving her personal courage and a confidence built from a series of successes.

Confidence is an ingredient in the recipe for success.

Barb Allen worked to build her own confidence through journaling, which helped her to process external feedback and internal reflection. A human resources consultant at Quaker pointed out to Allen that her colleagues consistently rated her performance very highly, while she gave herself lower scores. Allen thought her "modesty" kept her from becoming arrogant and focused her on how to improve. The consultant, however, advised Allen that if she continually discounted her own point of view, then she would be less likely to speak out and contribute as fully as she could.

How did Allen help herself to evaluate situations and focus on the positives of her own performance and the environment? She began journaling. The act of capturing situations on paper forced her to reflect on feedback and the results of her actions. Therefore, even if her point was not accepted in a meeting, she could think about what she learned or share her feelings. The journal helped her to put positives and negatives in perspective. It gave her the reinforcement she needed to move forward more confidently.

While you can develop confidence in your abilities as an adult, many of today's top female leaders developed self-confidence through their upbringings. Commander Barbara Scholley was taught that if she worked hard enough and wanted something badly enough, she could achieve her objective. She saw no indications, from her earliest memories of childhood in the Midwest, that women didn't have the same abilities and opportunities as did men. Similarly, for Sheri Wilson-Gray, her parents' belief in her translated into her own belief in herself. Today's leaders typically were raised with high expectations, and those expectations translated into confidence and a drive to succeed.

Act with Integrity

IT SOUNDS CLICHÉ, but when all is said and done, the only thing you really have is your own personal ethics. That value system helps you to set the right course in any endeavor, including your professional life. It is your beacon in good times, and most importantly, your guide in tough times.

Your integrity will be measured and tested every day—whether you are in the workforce or home with your kids. If you lie about your children's ages at the movie theater, you not only devalue your word but also teach a terrible lesson. At work, if your team sees you mislead the plant or misrepresent your product to customers, they will question everything you do.

Never compromise your integrity or the way you treat other human beings. Then you will be respected, and people will be able to rely upon your word. If you tell someone you'll support them, then you need to do it in the room with the CEO, even if the CEO doesn't support the point. Do not leave people out on a limb. Your word is everything.

A strong sense of ethics provides you with the solid base to act on the courage of your convictions. When Cynthia Round started at Ogilvy & Mather, she felt compelled to turn down her very first assignment. Round came to the advertising agency from Procter & Gamble, where she had worked on the Pampers business. Consequently, she had Pampers' next five-year plan in her head. When she was asked to work on the Huggies account for Ogilvy & Mather, she recognized that she was not comfortable using her knowledge of Pampers against Procter & Gamble in her new job. Although she was brand new to the agency, Round communicated her concern to the management team at Ogilvy & Mather. They respected both Round and her decision, and she was immediately reassigned.

If people don't trust you, nothing else matters. Business is transacted based on relationships, which in turn are based on respect and trust. Without those items, little can be accomplished. In the previous example, Cynthia Round showed from the get-go at Ogilvy & Mather that she had a well-developed sense of right and wrong and the courage of her convictions. The trust she engendered through turning down the Huggies assignment actually provided her with valuable currency for moving forward successfully. From the outset, she earned the trust and respect of her colleagues. They knew at once that she was a stand-up player.

Every day we read in the newspaper about someone who

loses sight of his or her values, becomes greedy, and tries to take a shortcut. Tales of insider trading, fraud, and theft are all too common. And, in the end, not only is it morally wrong, but it is also bad business. You will ruin your career and your life with these illicit shortcuts. Recently, I read about a "bright" young investment banker in Morgan Stanley Dean Witter's San Francisco office. Before he had even begun his job, which would pay him close to six figures with bonuses, he had rigged a scheme to share stock tips with a friend. After leaving the highlighted record of his trades on the copy machine, he was fired and is now sought by the FBI. If he had acted with integrity, he would have been a fast-track twenty-four-year-old with a great job, plenty of spending money, and his whole life before him. Instead, if convicted, he'll have a criminal record and little access to the kinds of lucrative jobs for which he had trained.

Acting with integrity is a long-term successful strategy.

Anyone, at any level of business, can succumb to greed and let personal integrity slip away. The 1999 conviction of Michael Andreas, son of the chairman of multinational Archer Daniels Midland, for price-fixing sent a promising senior manager to jail rather than to the executive suite. People in powerful positions sometimes forget that no one is above the law.

We are called upon all day long to make decisions that require judgment and a strong value system. However, not all situations are clear. Many fall in that murky gray area that is harder to evaluate. When you find yourself confronted by a conundrum, take a step back and try to reason your way through it. There are simple guideposts to help you. Would you be proud to share with a spouse, child, parent, or friend the actions you contemplate? Would you be comfortable if these actions were written about in the newspaper? If the answer to either of these questions is no, then pause for further reflection before moving forward. You may be in a trouble spot.

Reach for additional resources when you are not certain about the ethics of a situation. Consulting family, friends, and colleagues with whom you are comfortable is one starting spot. A mentor is another. And many companies have an ethics committee and guidelines to help their employees navigate potentially tricky paths. For example, General Motors has strict rules regarding the business conduct of its in-house money managers, who are responsible for the investment of billions of dollars of corporate assets. Those managers may not accept meals or gifts from anyone. If you run a real estate investment fund and are trying to establish a relationship with the managers from General Motors, you cannot "wine and dine" them. While a certain amount of socializing is part of doing business, the General Motors employees must pay their own way. Increasingly common in the last decade, strict guidelines help companies such as General Motors ensure that its employees, making important investment and other decisions, are not swayed by factors that do not directly influence return on their investment. These employers are trying to do away with the ethically gray areas.

Acting with integrity is a long-term successful strategy. Generally, good things happen to good people. That is why Alison Ressler, a partner at Sullivan & Cromwell, advises, "Do the right things personally and professionally. Try to be honest and up front. Set realistic expectations, and don't surprise people. Don't let your goals get out ahead of you.

Alison Ressler

A LISON WAS BORN in 1958 in New York City and has a younger sister. Alison's parents instilled in her a desire for success. When she was little, she wanted to be a teacher, so her mom said, "You'll start as a teacher, and then you'll be the principal." She attended an all-girls school through tenth grade, and was a top student. By eleventh grade, it didn't occur to her to do anything other than be at the top of her class.

Alison graduated from Brown University Phi Beta Kappa in 1980, and from Columbia Law School in 1983 where she met her husband. After school, both initially settled into jobs in New York but then Alison's husband accepted a position in Los Angeles. Alison's mentor at Milbank Tweed Hadley & McCoy advised her to try the new Sullivan & Cromwell Los Angeles office, and she started there as a junior associate in 1984. For four years, Alison was the only female lawyer. She has since risen from associate to partner in her firm.

Alison always knew she wanted a big family, and she and her husband have four children. Two were born while she was an associate and two while she was a partner. To help keep the household organized, Alison has nanny and housekeeping help. Her husband, who is now in business for himself, contributes on the domestic side.

Ressler serves on the Board of Advisors for Columbia Law School and on the Board of Directors of Laurence 2000, a private elementary school.

Do the best you can at your job, and maintain your integrity. Then, if you are liked, the rest will fall into place."

Take Your Reputation Seriously

YOUR REPUTATION—THE public "rap" about who you are—needs to be taken seriously. Seek to be known for your competence, likable personality, and integrity. A reputation for these qualities will ensure that people want to work with you. And attracting the best people to work with, that is, a strong team, will make your work life both more enjoyable and more productive. It's preferable for people to enjoy working with you rather than fear you. In fact, rule by fear is often used by those who lack confidence to bring others along in a more participatory, open environment.

You build your reputation with every interaction, no matter how casual. In a "small world," that impression can carry from one field to another. Your reputation does often travel before you. So remember, you are "on stage" all the time, and view every contact as an opportunity to make a good impression.

REGARDING values, Suzanne Nora Johnson passes on this advice from her parents, "Know what values are important and live to them regardless of the business, career, and financial impact. Reexamine your values regularly to be sure you are true to them."

You start building your reputation the first day you walk in the door. First impressions are powerful. It is far better to be thoughtful regarding your first impression than to put yourself in a situation of having to labor to change those impressions. While first impressions are made almost instantaneously, it can take many months of work to correct misperceptions. Therefore, take care up front.

In addition to being known as talented, likable, and having a strong sense of integrity, seek to be recognized as a hard worker. Your colleagues don't want to think they have added a slacker to their team. Notice what time people arrive and leave, and strive to be one of the first to arrive, but not one of the first to depart. I certainly am not an advocate of "face time"—staying at work just to be seen—but I do believe in sending the right message. And the right message, for someone at a new job or company, is to let others know that you are a dedicated, hard-working, team player. Additionally, when you start a new job, there is a lot to be learned. You can't possibly be operating at maximum efficiency. Therefore, being extra diligent and spending some additional hours up front will be noticed and appreciated. Once you have hit your stride, you can tailor your schedule as appropriate.

🖋 POWER POINTER *Use an honest assessment of your own strengths and weaknesses to your advantage. The fact that men rarely express their uncertainty or admit doubt, e.g., won't ask for directions, often helps them in a professional environment. However, women can combat that advantage by making their willingness to recognize personal strengths and weaknesses an even stronger asset. Seek jobs and assignments that play to your strengths, and in a team environment, complement your weaknesses through the skills of your colleagues.*

CHAPTER NINE SUMMARY AT-A-GLANCE

Use the checklist below to make sure you understand the points and steps discussed in chapter nine.

Know yourself.
- ☑ Honestly assess your values.
- ☑ Truthfully determine your skill set, likes, dislikes, and style.
- ☑ Seek feedback from others, including professionals.

Be yourself.
- ☑ Know that being yourself is the only sustainable strategy.
- ☑ Don't change to fit someone else's mold or standards.
- ☑ Address the narrower band of acceptable business behavior for women.

Have confidence in yourself.
- ☑ Your belief in yourself is an ingredient for success.
- ☑ You can develop confidence in a professional environment.

Act with integrity.
- ☑ Have the courage of your convictions.
- ☑ Hold to your values.
- ☑ Seek guidance in the "gray areas."

Take your reputation seriously.
- ☑ Build your reputation with every encounter.
- ☑ Create strong first impressions.

Never Accept No
for an Answer

❧ POWER POINTER   *Don't let obstacles derail you.*

"A DIAMOND IS a piece of coal that stuck with the job,"
said my fortune cookie one evening. That sage advice
was echoed throughout my interviews with today's top
business leaders. These women distinguish themselves, not
only through their abilities to communicate, solve problems,
lead and contribute to a team, but also through their tenacity. They refuse to be derailed from an objective. They will
not take no for an answer.

Staying the course is something we are all capable of.
You don't have to be the smartest person or have the best
pedigree—even to make it all the way to the top. We all have
it within ourselves to be tenacious, if we choose to be. What
are the core components of tenacity that can help you reach
your objective? Appropriate expectations, belief in yourself,
a strong work ethic, resilience, and persistence.

Develop Appropriate Expectations

EXPECTATIONS HAVE A lot to do with the staying power required to rise through an organization or run your own business. As we've seen in the examples throughout this book, women who became leaders expected to work hard and were not put off by that necessity. In fact, they thrived on the challenges. The women "pioneers" who entered the work force or completed business school in the 1970s could see clearly that they were unique—as there were few other women around—and, therefore, they expected to work hard to surmount obstacles. They did not compromise or adjust their expectations downward in any way, but they did expect to encounter turbulence as they sought their business and professional objectives.

For instance, when Lillian Kraemer was in law school in the early sixties, she assumed becoming a lawyer as a female would be hard, so she was not derailed when it was. Kraemer was one of 7 women out of 175 students in her University of Chicago Law School class. Kraemer notes that today's women law students, in classes that are approximately 50 percent female, often don't see that the business world is still male-dominated, and therefore they are hit harder by perceived unfairness in the professional environment.

When Kraemer returned to law school following her first year, she expectantly approached her Law Review desk. A large New York law firm regularly placed invitations to interview on the desks of the top fifteen students by grades (Law Review). In this particular year (1962), there were only fourteen invitations—in spite of the fact that Kraemer was actually number one in the class. Today, the obstacles women face are substantially more subtle. You likely will receive the interview and, perhaps, the job. But you may not get the plum assignments with the most important clients. Don't be satisfied with that. Do your job well, and speak up for what you think you deserve. Once you've achieved it, you've helped yourself and others.

A long-term perspective can help you stay the course through good times and bad. Again, expectations are important. If you expect immediate gratification—promotions, glamorous responsibilities, and financial reward—you may be sorely disappointed. It takes time to learn a business, develop contacts, and lay the groundwork for real success.

CONNIE Duckworth's father provided her with essential business advice: "It takes ten years to build a base." When she graduated college, that seemed like an eternity—half her lifetime. But now, from her vantage point as a managing director at Goldman Sachs and CEO of MuniGroup.com—she has seen that it is true. Duckworth affirms, "It takes a while to gain expertise and learn to handle things. Don't expect all to go perfectly, and don't sweat the small stuff. Keep your eye on long-term opportunities."

Believe in Yourself

A POSITIVE MENTAL attitude goes a long way to help you solve problems and succeed in your objectives. It usually goes hand-in-hand with a belief in yourself—a belief that if you go about something in a smart fashion and work hard enough at it, you will accomplish your objective. Self-confidence, discussed in chapter nine, is an important element of belief in yourself.

Janet Gurwitch Bristow's belief in herself and refusal to take no for an answer helped her secure a job at Foley's department store after she received a rejection letter. "Pursue your goals with energy, optimism, and creativity, but pursue, pursue, pursue," says Gurwitch Bristow, who followed this advice, with a little guidance from her father, as she sought her first job out of college. Gurwitch Bristow was interested in retail and interviewed with a number of companies, but her primary objective was to obtain a position at Foley's, the strongest regional chain of department stores based in Houston.

> *A positive mental attitude goes a long way to help you solve problems and succeed in your objectives.*

As a senior at the University of Alabama in 1974, Gurwitch Bristow sent her resume to Foley's but was crestfallen to receive a reply stating that Foley's did not hire from her school. When she discussed her disappointment with her father, he advised, "That's ridiculous. Present yourself in person, and show them what you can do. They'll never remember sending you the letter." And Janet did. She was hired and spent eighteen extremely successful years with Foley's, rising to senior vice president and becoming one of two women on Foley's board of directors.

Today, Gurwitch Bristow still keeps Foley's original rejection letter in her desk. She explains, "There will always be people trying to derail you or not believing in you. You have to believe in yourself, be tenacious, and pursue your goals."

Develop Stamina and a Strong Work Ethic

WORK ETHIC AND stamina are part and parcel of a leader's drive for success. Your work ethic will take you the distance, but you need stamina to get there. While there are many attributes that can speed your trip to the top—or to wherever you aspire to go—a strong work ethic is imperative. If you're comfortable with the other qualities we've already discussed in this book, then applying them through a strong work ethic can catapult you to the apex. Even if you lack a fancy pedigree or membership in Mensa—the exclusive club for geniuses—hard work can be a great equalizer or distinguishing factor. A strong work ethic yields rich results.

"Work ethic has driven my success more than anything else," comments Valerie Salembier, the publisher of *Esquire*. Throughout her career, Salembier has routinely worked long hours. And that hard work has helped her get through some difficult spots. In response to a job in a highly political environment Salembier adopted the mantra "nose to the grindstone." She's since found this to be a useful focusing tool for both political situations and disappointments. Salembier learned that if you let politics get to you, your performance is negatively impacted. In those situations, her mantra reminds her that she is paid to do a job, not worry about rumors. It helps her focus on what matters and puts her back on track.

A strong work ethic yields rich results.

When Salembier is faced with disappointments, such as not winning business that she has worked for, rather than become upset, she thinks, "Nose to the grindstone. How can I go back to the client and try again to win the account?" The mantra prods Salembier to remember that the situation in question is not about her, which remove her own emotions from the problem and refocuses her on business.

Alison Ressler, partner at law firm Sullivan & Cromwell, balances family life with what she terms her "extreme dedication to what she does." For example, for four months, she represented the thrift H. F. Ahmanson in its unsuccessful attempt to take over Great Western. Throughout the process, she and her client spoke twice daily and once on weekends. In those four months, she missed only one call (when in Peru). She was on conference calls from airports, or wherever she was. At the conclusion of the effort, her client commented that he could not have gotten a higher level of dedication and service. That level of commitment sets Ressler apart from others.

Work ethic is a key driver of success in any environment. Commander Barbara Scholley faced two daunting challenges in her first assignment as an electrical officer in the navy. First, she had no technical background, and second, she was the rare female manager in a hardcore male environment. Specifically, Scholley was twenty-three years old and living

Your work ethic will take you the distance, but you need stamina to get there.

away from home, in Charleston, South Carolina, for the first time. As a biology major with a strong science orientation and a love of the water, Scholley had thought the navy would offer an interesting career path. However, as a recent graduate of Officer Candidate School, she found herself assigned in an area in which she had no technical expertise, to super-

Barbara L. Scholley

B OBBIE IS THE middle child of three daughters and has a brother twenty years younger. She was the family tomboy and loved to help her dad, a State Farm employee, on their boat. Bobbie's mom, who hadn't attended college and worked as a beautician, felt like she missed out without a career or education. Bobbie wanted to chart a different path, and she felt comfortable doing so. She was taught that if she went after something with hard work, she could achieve her objective.

In 1980, Bobbie received her BS in biology from Illinois State University. She joined the U.S. Navy and was commissioned in May 1981 through Officer Candidate School. Between 1981 and 1990, Bobbie held several positions, including electrical officer, diving officer, repair services officer, navigator, navigation piloting instructor and Ninth Company officer, operations officer and navigator aboard the USS *Vulcan,* executive officer of the USS *Hoist,* and commander of the USS *Bolster* from October 1992 until decommissioning in September 1994. She was the fourth woman to take command of a U.S. Navy ship.

Following her successful command of the USS *Bolster,* Bobbie served as senior diving officer during the four-month salvage of TWA Flight 800 and was the first woman to be assigned as the supervisor of diving for the entire U.S. Navy. She has received numerous decorations and commendations.

Bobbie is married to Frank Scholley, an engineering consultant and product developer and former Navy SEAL.

vise fifty men who ranged from eighteen- year-old kids straight out of boot camp to her assistant, a master chief with thirty years of navy experience.

How did Barbara Scholley not only "survive" but thrive in these circumstances? She did what it took. She explains, "I was taught growing up that if I was willing to work hard and wanted something badly enough, I could accomplish it. So I worked long hours both learning the engineering piece and running the division." Scholley's days began at 7 A.M. and often didn't finish until 9 or 10 P.M. In addition, every third day, including weekends, she was "on duty" for twenty-four hours. And because her division's job was to repair submarines, as problems arose, her team dealt with them regardless of the day or hour. Scholley comments, "There's a navy saying—a half workday is twelve hours; a full day is twenty-four."

As a young woman working to overcome the skepticism of many of the men she supervised, Scholley's challenges were magnified, for she had to prove that she could do the job as well as a man. Scholley notes, "I rolled up my sleeves to get dirty side by side with the men. I earned the professional respect of my coworkers and subordinates because of my competence and hard work."

If you love your job and other responsibilities, you will be happy to get up and get started on your day.

How do you build the stamina required to juggle the many different aspects of your life and to succeed in your career? First, your energy level is directly influenced by your excitement regarding the activities in which you are engaged. If you love your job and other responsibilities, you will be happy to get up and get started on your day. On the other hand, if you are not motivated and stimulated by those activities, you will experience a lower energy level and less desire to move forward. Second, take care of yourself. While it sounds easy, as we're all pulled in many directions, often the last person to be considered is "me." Inevitably, you will make many trade-offs, but one of them cannot be your health. Make sure that your body and soul are getting the nourishment they need to enable you to operate at maximum efficiency and capacity. That means getting the sleep that your body requires, developing healthy eating habits, drinking lots of water (rather than caffeinated drinks), and exercising as regularly as possible. Being mentally and physically alert gives you an edge.

Your goals can help you "stay the course" in good times, and, especially, in bad.

Cultivate Resilience

CLIMBING THE LADDER has challenges at every level, and for everyone. Even those who move forward with apparent ease face difficulties, many of which may not be seen by the casual observer. Paula Sneed believes, "You are not measured by promotions or articles in the newspaper, but when you are passed over or fired. That shows your mettle." She counsels, "At first one's resilience is not good, then it gets better. The challenge is to minimize the time in the trough. That shows resilience and resourcefulness."

Your goals can help you "stay the course" in good times and, especially, in bad. When you are disappointed, it's easy to let your emotions cloud your judgment regarding what's best for you. Instead, take time to step back and "cool off" before acting. There were a number of situations in Paula Sneed's career when she wanted something that didn't happen right away or even at all. Rather than react emotionally or impulsively when confronted with unsettling news, Sneed doesn't respond immediately. Instead, she takes time to reflect—for a day or longer—until she feels she can be more objective and consider the big picture. In contrast, you probably have seen people leave a company after one seemingly bad event—such as someone getting promoted instead of them. Often, the disappointing circumstance results from an "environmental situation" that isn't about them. But they don't see that. Nor are they around to know that they would have been better off had they stayed.

Be Persistent

"WINNERS NEVER QUIT, and quitters never win." So yelled a tennis coach as he hit balls to me at each end of the court. The saying stuck in my mind then, and it has remained with me since. It summarizes the persistence required to make it to the top in today's business environment.

Tenacity is a particularly valuable quality in difficult situations. "Anyone can be fine when the water is calm. But in order to withstand the storm, you need strong stuff in you," says Phyllis Apelbaum, an avid sailor. Apelbaum exhibited her strong stuff when she decided to start her own company in 1974. Striking out to open her own messenger service, a business she had worked in for many years, she took all of a recently bequeathed $3,500 inheritance—her entire savings—and applied for the necessary ICC license from the

Paula Sneed

PAULA WAS BORN in 1947 and raised in a working-class town outside of Boston. She was extremely close to her extended family, and as an only child, she found her parents poured their resources and aspirations on her. Paula was one of seven African American children in her high school class of six hundred, and she experienced firsthand the process of desegregation and the fight for equal rights. These events inspired Paula to set her sights high and to try to make things better for others in the future.

Paula learned many important lessons from her parents, both of whom were high school graduates. From her mom, she learned activism and leadership because her mom worked in a city government office and was deeply involved in the community. The fact that her mom worked also taught Paula independence and that if she wanted something, she had to earn it. From her dad, a transit worker, she learned about determination and how to reach her goals.

Paula graduated with a BA from Simmons College in 1969 and worked in the nonprofit world. She received her MBA from Harvard University in 1977 and joined General Foods Corporation (now part of Kraft) as an assistant product manager. Her product management experience includes both established brands and new product activities. In 1986, she was appointed vice president, consumer affairs. In 1990 she was named senior vice president, GF USA and president of the food service division. In 1991, Paula became executive vice president of GF USA and general manager of the desserts division. In 1995, following the merger of Kraft and General Foods, she became senior vice president of marketing services for Kraft Foods, and in 1999 she was named executive vice president of Kraft Foods and president of the e-commerce division.

Paula, who has received numerous awards and has been profiled in a multitude of media, is a member of the board of directors of Hercules Incorporated, Airgas Inc., and Westchester/Fairfield Inroads. She's on the advisory council to the Dean of Howard University Business School; and she's a member of the Executive Leadership Council; the National Association of Negro Business and Professional Women; Coalition of 100 Black Women; the Association of American University Women, and the Women's Forum.

Paula, who is married to a consultant and has one daughter, commutes back and forth between their New Jersey home and Kraft's Illinois headquarters.

Phyllis Apelbaum

PHYLLIS GREW UP as the oldest of six children in a family without many resources. Consequently, a high school education was not possible, and Phyllis began working at thirteen. Her "saving grace" was her love of books, which she devoured and used to educate herself.

Phyllis began amassing her nascent business skills as a fourteen-year-old Jewish girl working with nuns at a hospital. One nun took her under her wing and taught her to run the switchboard—even though switchboard operators were supposed to be at least seventeen. This vital skill enabled her to move on to serve as an order taker at American United Cab Company. There, someone thought it would be "cute" to teach a young girl to be a dispatcher, which gave her yet another skill. She learned to process thousands of taxi orders in an eight-hour shift, and she learned how to teach others those skills. Wanting to shift from a night job to day work, Apelbaum moved to a messenger service. In 1974, the company she worked for was sold, and Apelbaum founded Arrow Messenger Service with her $3,500 inheritance. Today, her company, of which she is chairman and CEO, is the largest female-owned messenger service in the Chicago area.

Phyllis is divorced and has a grown son and two grandsons.

Illinois License Bureau. The bureau eventually denied her application seventeen times because they would not grant a woman the required license, and after the last application Apelbaum was broke. Frustrated and upset, she spied the commissioner's office and stormed in to confront him with the fact that she had been denied all those times and yet he hadn't ever attended a hearing. The commissioner, a man of integrity and now a long-time friend of Apelbaum's, finally helped to right the situation and set Apelbaum on her way. Had Apelbaum given up, she would never have realized her dream of having her own company.

Persistence is one of Rose Marie Bravo's key attributes. She keeps at something until she is able to make it happen. She counsels, "You may have to accept a 'no,' but it doesn't mean it's never going to happen. Think, maybe I'll come back at it another time, another way. Eventually, you get everything you want." You may recall from chapter five that it took Bravo and her team two years of effort to secure the Prada line for Saks Fifth Avenue. Her persistence kept Saks from missing a significant opportunity—monetarily and strategically—and

TENACITY can help you with elaborate objectives and relatively simple ones, too. At a former employer, Carole Black wanted new computers for her department. She approached person after person until finally someone said, "My gosh, she must really need them. Give her the computers, and get her off my back." But success only happened after her tenth request.

moved Saks one large step closer to realizing its corporate vision.

POWER POINTER Don't let obstacles derail you. Know that there will be bumps in the road and adjust your expectations to include them. While men and women both face ups and downs during the course of a career, for women, in what is still a male-dominated work environment, the obstacles may be larger and more frequent. Don't be defeated by them. Instead, learn and grow stronger. As Phyllis Apelbaum notes, "When all else fails, put your right foot in your right shoe, your left foot in your left shoe, and move your feet, one step at a time, one in front of the other. You will get where you're destined to be."

CHAPTER TEN SUMMARY AT-A-GLANCE

Use the checklist below to make sure you understand the points and steps discussed in chapter ten.

Develop appropriate expectations.
- ☑ Keep expectations high, and know that there will be bumps in the road, but don't let the difficulties derail you.
- ☑ Take the long view.

Believe in yourself.
- ☑ Belief in your own ability to succeed helps you to stick with a plan and achieve your objectives.

Develop stamina and a strong work ethic.
- ☑ Distinguish yourself from among a crowded field with your work ethic.
- ☑ Nourish your body and your soul.
- ☑ Achieve rich results through hard work and dedication.

Cultivate resilience.
- ☑ Minimize your time in the trough and learn from it.
- ☑ Recognize when you should "stay the course."

Be persistent.
- ☑ Never accept no for an answer.

Having It All

G OSH, I'M SO glad this isn't a 'have it all' book," said
Mary Baglivo, mother of two young children, when
I interviewed her. Nonetheless, as she too acknowledges, trying to "have it all" is an issue that cannot be
ignored when considering women, success, and business.

Can you "have it all"? And what is "having it all"? There
are a plethora of opinions—even among the uniformly accomplished group of leaders interviewed for *The New Success
Rules for Women*. In this chapter, I provide you with strategies
to define and achieve your personal version of having it all.

What Is Having It All?

"HAVING IT ALL" is different for each individual. It is
deeply personal and only by knowing yourself, your values,
your dreams, and your realities can you know what it means
for you. For some, having it all may be having a few highly

cherished things; for others it may be a long litany of items. One woman might seek to have a high-powered business career and to give back through community service. Another might seek to pay the bills with her income and otherwise to maximize time spent with family. Traditionally "having it all" has referred to having a rewarding job and an active family life. Today, however, it can mean almost anything. The key is to identify and to have in your life those essential elements that make you happy. Try committing to paper just what those critical components are for you.

"Having it all" does not necessarily mean striving to reach the top of your professional field. While this book is dedicated to helping you go as fast and as far as your talent and interest allow, it's important to stress that it's okay not to want to reach the top. Societal expectation often makes it seem like anything less than striving to be number one is cause for con-

What is critical is to know what's important to you, and to reach for that.

cern, but it's not. It's fine if you seek the top, and it's great, too, if you don't. What is critical is to know what's important to you, and to reach for that. Don't try to live up to the expectations of your parents, boyfriend, girlfriend, spouse, boss, or someone else you are trying to please. Achieve for yourself.

Can You Have It All?

WHETHER OR NOT you can have it all depends on you— on how you define that goal and, just as importantly, on your time frame. When I asked today's most successful female business leaders whether it was possible to have it all, they were divided in their responses. A significant percentage said no, you can't have it all—you have to make choices. An equally large percentage said yes, you can have it all—but you have to make choices. While their answers seem contradictory, the common thread is choices. To make sense of the contradiction, you need to return to your definition of success and having it all.

If your definition of having it all is enjoying a satisfying relationship with your significant other, playing a primary role in raising your family, climbing the corporate ladder with great speed, taking a leadership role in the civic arena, maintaining fabulous relationships with a wide circle of friends and making new ones as well, pursuing hobbies, taking care of yourself through regular exercise and grooming, and reading good books, then it may not be possible—not all at the same time. The limiting factor, of course, is that there is only one of you. You can only be in one place at a time, and you can only give one thing at a time your undivided attention. However, there is a second, critical dimension to having it all—time frame. Over what period of time do you need to have it all?

The Importance of Time Frame

IF YOU SEEK to have it all on a daily, weekly, monthly, or even annual basis, then your chance of "having it all" is small. However, if you examine that question over a decade or a lifetime, your chances improve significantly. Think about time frame in relation to the definition of "all" that I just described above. No human being could accomplish all those agendas on a daily, weekly, or monthly basis. Stretch that to a year and possibly a small number of superwomen could do it. However, examine a five- to ten-year period or consider your objectives over a lifetime, and suddenly you have a chance to accomplish all those things.

Recognizing that you have choices is empowering, but the key is action.

Just as your definition of having it all is personal, so too is figuring out what time frame is right for you. The key, once again, is knowing and being honest with yourself. And, again, it may help to explore these issues by committing your professional and personal goals to paper, with time frames attached.

How will you know if you have things "organized" the right way for you? Listen to your heart, and listen to your body. If you are at equilibrium, you will experience ups and downs—we all do—but overall, you will feel good about who you are, where you are, and what you are doing. If things are out of kilter, on the other hand, you may feel extraordinarily stressed, tired, depressed, sad, confused, or just plain unhappy. You may be short-tempered, you may have trouble focusing, and you may be overwhelmed. Of course, it's natural in today's fast-paced world to experience some of these feelings some of the time. But if such feelings persist, it's time to reexamine your priorities and choices. Just recognizing that you have choices is empowering, but the key is action.

Take Control

TAKING CONTROL MEANS recognizing and acting upon your responsibility to make choices for yourself—that

Robin Foote

ROBIN, BORN IN 1945, is the second of three daughters in her family. Her father was a role model, as were several of his friends and other colleagues she met during the course of her career. She graduated from Smith College in 1967 and Harvard Business School in 1969, where she was the first female to be named a Baker Scholar. In 1994, she summed up the first 25 years of her career in a poem for her HBS class reunion:

The Road to Wisdom

Together again, after 25 years;
Time to recall the joy, the tears.
Left HBS eager, all full of hope,
Terribly naïve, ill-prepared to cope.
To tell it all, some pride I must swallow.
Recall trails blazed for those who would follow.
Business was not ready for women in our day.
Limited our choices, affecting our pay.
But that's all changed now. Old wounds have healed.
Time to look back. Time events were revealed.
Out on my own, heading into the fray—
Joined McKinsey, expecting to stay.
But after nine years—denied partnership twice—
Learned the rules of the game are not always nice.
Four years at Levi's were enough for me.
Returned to Chicago, to FNBC.
I've mentored young people coming behind.
Helped them succeed as they move up the line.

Yes, I've paid quite a price, hit some brick walls.
Taken my lumps, had my share of falls.
But I've always come back. I'm not a quitter.
Learned what I could. Emerged that much fitter.
Driving me forward, on toward the top,
Is a pioneer spirit that won't let me stop.
And while it hasn't been all work and no play,
I must admit, it started that way.
Working so hard, I could finally see
I was taking myself far too seriously!
Since lightening up, loosening the rein,
I'm hearing birds, smelling flowers again.
I'm in a new role—an exciting fresh start—
Doing my bit; having fun with my part.
Still working hard, but playing lots more,
Enjoying the game, not keeping score.
Material needs met, close friends to treasure.
It comes down to this: Life's now a pleasure!
This story I've told because it's the truth
Of one woman's journey toward wisdom from youth.
                              —M.R.F. May 1994

In 1997, Robin joined Bank of America as Group Executive Vice President, only to find herself replaced by a NationsBank executive at the time of the merger. In 1998, she started Randolph Partners, a consulting company.

Robin is single and enjoys hiking, camping, skiing, music, art, and reading. She is a director of DLJ*direct*, and former director of the Community Investment Corporation, the Juvenile Diabetes Foundation (Chicago Chapter), Leadership Greater Chicago, the HBS Alumni Board, Music of the Baroque, and several other organizations.

includes small choices as well as big "life" choices. As we saw in chapter two, Robin Foote's decisions have not always been conscious. As she became deeply involved in her career, she made choices that, by default, became important decisions regarding personal relationships and family. Robin comments, "I've always tended to commit to excess, and this was certainly true of my early career. I've learned, however, that you need to ask yourself why you are in it and make sure you are satisfied with the price you are paying. Be realistic. It is easy to incrementalize your way along. Look and reflect early." Foote believed for many years that it was professionally risky to cut back. Recently, however, when she has done just that, she has achieved at least as much success. Foote adds, "Stay aware. Nurture ways that take you away from the immediate stresses and that allow you to gain perspective and make conscious choices."

Choice is power. The fact that you can choose your path carries with it the responsibility to do so. Don't let things "happen to you." Don't be a victim. Instead, take charge, and work to make your goals a reality. You will be more likely to achieve success if you have identified some fundamental macro objectives. To help you consider the multidimensional facets of your life, use the seven spheres approach described in chapter two. And, again, layer in your time frame. Consider the different phases of your life and what may be important to you at each point. When you have completed that exercise, you are less likely to make so many incremental decisions that you wind up someplace you don't want to be.

Recognize That Your Choices Have Consequences

IT'S A CLICHÉ, but it's true: Life is a series of trade-offs. As one objective takes priority, another necessarily slips back. If earning the next promotion becomes your number one goal, then as a consequence, other items fall in relative rank. If helping your child through a difficult time becomes your number one priority, then earning that promotion may fall to number two (or lower). While you still may achieve both objectives, number two becomes less likely than if it were number one. And certainly there is no guarantee you'll succeed at your number one objective either, but likelihood increases if it is a real number one—in actions as well as words.

A helpful exercise to see if your actions are consistent with your ideals involves the following steps: (1) write out what is important to you in priority order; (2) when you have completed that list, write down how you allocate your time; and (3) compare the two lists. Do your actions match your intentions? Of course, some commitments, such as full-time employment, have defined minimum requirements. Consider your time overall as well as how you use your disposable time—what's left over after sleep and other basics.

Trade-offs are personal and must reflect your own values. Trade-offs made by the women I interviewed range from sleep, exercise, and hobbies to friends, marriage, and children. Barb Allen trades off everything but work and family. By prioritizing down to two things that are critical to her, she is able to focus her attention on them and, by her definition, have it all. Allen is not casual about what she takes on or gives up. She brings laser focus to both. When I interviewed her, I was able to fill an entire page with the things that she trades off, including friends, community service, hobbies, and exercise. That works just fine for her, but it also may change over time. Allen's oldest child recently left for college, so shortly she may be able to reallocate her time and get to some of the items that, for many years, she has traded off.

Indra Nooyi has made a professional trade-off, although she is still at the top of her field. So she can spend more time with her two children, she has traded having a line position at PepsiCo—that would enable her to run a large business but that would require significant travel—for her role as senior vice president of corporate strategy and development and CFO. Similarly, after Tanya Mandor missed her daughter's first birthday because she was in Hong Kong, she gave up working in the ready-to-wear business, which required substantial travel—often out of the country—and

SUE Kronick and many others I interviewed traded off having children in order to focus on their careers. Kronick, for example, did not think it was possible to "have it all" and not feel guilty. She notes, "Some say, 'I'd rather feel guilty and tired and have all these things.' You just need to choose. You only go around once, so make a conscious decision." Kronick made her choices and considers herself lucky. She is married to an incredibly supportive man with his own career. Together, they work and play hard and have a vigorous life. It is what Kronick wants.

almost left retail altogether. While ultimately cosmetics proved at least as exciting to Mandor, at the time she was not certain it would. Given the circumstances in which she found herself, Mandor made a choice—to put family first— and traded off an existing job in which she excelled.

"Balance" Is a Faulty Objective

NOW THAT WE'VE touched upon choices, where does the concept of balance fit in? How about the often-discussed question, Can you balance your drive for professional success with non-work interests? Although there are entire books written on the topic of how to do just that, I think balance is a concept that is fraught with difficulties in this context. Balance is a tension-producing state. Therefore, if you seek to create balance, you diminish your chances of success, not just with a particular objective, but also with those items that you seek to balance.

Few things in this world are truly stable, including the demands of your job or your family. Therefore, in order to succeed, you need to be able to adjust how you allocate your energy over increments of time. As in your professional life, you need to have flexibility built into your "system." Balance, in the purest sense of the term, makes that more difficult.

Barb Allen has things organized in a way that's right for her, but on any given day, it can feel imbalanced. On some days she feels out of control, and on others, she feels cool— that everything is going great. The out-of-control days occur when there are competing demands from so many constituencies that inevitably Allen feels like she is letting someone down who is important to her. For example, if her daughter's soccer game is at 2:30 in the afternoon (because inevitably they are), then she needs to leave her office at 1:15 to commute to the match. But, the phone might ring at 1:05 with an important call, so she runs out at 1:25. Then she's stopped in the hall by a colleague and really leaves at 1:35. After driving madly, she arrives to discover that the game has been moved to a different field, and so she misses it. Other events that can lead to that out-of-control feeling include childcare breakdowns and school schedule changes. There is no average day.

Blend: An Alternative to Balance

WHAT, THEN, IS an alternate, more effective concept than balance? Blend. Blending implies a coming together and mixing. It is more fluid and, therefore, can change more easily over time.

This isn't just a question of semantics. Rather, it is an approach to enable you to accomplish a number of objectives over time in discreet areas of your life. It is an approach that recognizes the changing demands from those areas. And it is an approach that builds in the flexibility to adjust your priorities—by changing the blend. Your needs vary over different phases of your life and even within those phases. Therefore, at different points in your life, you will have different blends. For example, when you've been given a big promotion at work, "blend" enables you to devote, for a period of time, greater resources to that part of your life. As a consequence, during that stage, you may have to rely on greater nanny

At different points in your life, you will have different blends.

help and/or contribution from your spouse. It is impossible to predict precisely how your life will unfold. The only certainty is that your blend will change over time.

Burnout Is Not an Efficient Solution

BURNOUT IS A negative consequence of pushing too hard simultaneously on too many fronts. Burnout occurs when you don't adequately prioritize. It happens when you don't recognize that lower priority items may have to drop off your list altogether. It happens when you don't say no. And, for many "hard-chargers," it's something that we think happens to other people—who may not be quite as strong. Sue Shellenbarger, a savvy journalist and mom, wrote compellingly about her firsthand experience with burnout in an essay titled, "No, You're Not Too Tough to Suffer a Bout of Burnout." It first appeared in the *Wall Street Journal* on June 25, 1997, and was included in her book, *Work & Family*.

Though I've written about burnout as a workplace issue, I secretly believed it was a malady suffered by others.

Studies have said as much as 25 percent of the work force is at risk of burnout. Nevertheless, I thought of the term as a pop-culture label for fatigue, or a scapegoat for bad work habits. With a flexible job I enjoy, I thought I was immune.

That's what I thought. And with that attitude I ran my life— straight into the ground.

In experiencing a bout with what I now respectfully call work-family burnout, I learned some things. Burnout is progressive; it sneaks up on you and, unchecked, gradually destroys your ability to see and solve problems. It's most likely to strike those who are doing something they perceive as important, and it undermines their ability to achieve it. At worst, burnout blacks out the most healing dimensions of life: self-awareness and closeness with others. Some notes on my experience, in hopes it might be helpful to others:

March: Spring brings a burst of energy, and I throw myself into a variety of roles, covering a spate of news, working on a new job project, managing my son's T-ball team, driving my daughter to soccer and volunteering at my kids' school (Colin Powell would be proud).

The phone rings nonstop, mail pours in, the fax bumps and grinds through the night. Enthused about everything I'm doing, I rise earlier and work later.

Early April: I begin misfiring at work. I send my usually receptive editor a column proposal and am startled to learn she finds it harebrained. I spend days interviewing experts for a story only to realize I can't use the information. Brain rot sets in. I call my boss to tell her about a new project; she listens patiently, then says, "You told me about that last week." I have no recollection.

Mid-April: To compensate for time poorly spent, I work longer and later. Sitting in my office, I doze off during phone calls. On the floor playing with my son one evening, reenacting the movie *Twister* with an imaginary tornado whipping through a play village, I fall asleep sitting up. By the time I awaken, the entire "village" is destroyed. I wonder what else I've been sleeping through.

Late April: Cherished family relationships start to suffer as the irritability and impatience symptomatic of burnout sets in. As I approach my son's room one night, he slams the door. "Mom, you yell too much," he calls from behind the door.

I haven't walked my dog in weeks, but I fail to notice that

the calm and perspective afforded by exercise are slipping away. My spiritual life atrophies; a phone message from my church, asking where I've been, sits on my desk.

Early May: My grim mood spills over to my daughter, who grows tense about school. Though I'm vaguely aware something is wrong, I can't see a way out.

I am startled to see out my window one evening dozens of artificial flowers sticking out of the ground. My son has "planted" them, creating a facsimile of the garden I haven't found time for. The fakes remind me I want a real garden, but I can't imagine when I might plant one.

Late May: After a month of minor illnesses, I raise a white flag and see my doctor. Hearing my pathetic litany of ailments, he eyes me askance and asks: "Don't you write about balancing work and family?" Get a grip, he orders: I'm burning out. (Though neither psychiatrists nor physicians include burnout in their listings of clinical ailments, I later learn, many use the term frequently in practice.) A false alarm—an X-ray showing what are later diagnosed as harmless lung abnormalities—provides another reality check. As my nine-year-old daughter, who has accompanied me, stares perplexed at the X-ray on my doctor's wall, I look at her and wonder, "What if this is all the time I have? Have I lived my life in the way that is best for her?"

Early June: Back in my office I call the man who coined the term burnout. Herbert Freudenberger, seventy, a Holocaust survivor, author and New York psychoanalyst who has been practicing for 40 years, experienced burnout in the 1960s, working in clinics providing free care to street people, and named it in the 1970s. The term has been overused and abused, he acknowledges. Nevertheless, he sees real burnout (a process brought about by excess demands on one's energy and coping mechanisms) as widespread, worsened by mass firings and disenchantment in the workplace. Also, jugglers like me trying to do too much.

Over the years, Dr. Freudenberger says, he has learned to hold burnout at bay. He stopped conducting seminars and agreeing to certain media appearances. His acid test for activity: If you had one more year to live, would you do it?

Then, "I draw the line," he says.

By Dr. Freudenberger's measure, I have a way to go in pruning my life. Humbled, I realize my kids will probably look back one day and laugh at me as an artifact of the baby boom age: someone trying to do it all, a cultural relic that will be as scorned in the future as multicolored shag rugs are now. Chalk it up to self-awareness.

For now, at least, I'm going to work right away on another remedy Dr. Freudenberger prescribes: closeness with others. If you'll excuse me, I'm off for a long weekend at the beach with my family.

Work Smart

YOU CAN RELIEVE stress, prevent burnout, and give "having it all" your best shot by working smart. Here are the nine strategies of working smart:

1. Prioritize and manage your time judiciously.
2. Learn to say no.
3. Organize through lists and other resources.
4. Multitask to increase efficiency.
5. Eliminate the guilt.
6. Recognize that personal success is a team effort.
7. Take time to recharge.
8. Step back regularly to review where you are.

9. Remember, you have choices and can change what isn't working.

Prioritize and Manage Your Time Judiciously

Prioritizing judiciously is central to managing your time and working both effectively and efficiently. Do you ever feel that you are running from one crisis to the next throughout your day—"putting out fires?" If the answer is yes, you may be particularly in need of a system for prioritizing. You need to break out of that pattern and take control—work on what is important, and not just what is urgent. That way, you will not get as caught up in the minutia of everyday business life, but instead you will be strategic about how you spend your time. One of the best systems for prioritizing is presented by Stephen Covey in *The 7 Habits of Highly Effective People.* Covey utilizes a two-dimensional framework to examine both the importance and urgency of an issue. I have adapted it below to address the topics covered in this book.

	URGENT	NOT URGENT
IMPORTANT	**Activities** • Crises • Immediate issues • Pressing projects central to your goals	**Activities** • Relationship-building— including through networks • Team-building • Personal development • Self-promotion • Strategic planning— personal and professional
NOT IMPORTANT	**Activities** • Interruptions, including some mail, e-mail and telephone calls • Some meetings that are not essential to contributing to your mission, values and goals	**Activities** • Non-essential mail, e-mail and telephone calls • Non-essential work

Your objective is to spend as much of your time as you can in quadrant two, where activities are important but not urgent. Those are the activities such as strategic planning, relationship building, preventive problem-solving, and recognizing new opportunities that lead to larger success and will over time minimize the size of quadrant one, which represents urgent and important activities. Quadrant one includes crises and deadline-driven projects—the fires we put out. Spending too much time there leads to going from one crisis to the next and is highly stressful, yet less effective as a long-term strategy. Additionally, you should minimize your time in quadrants three and four, as those quadrants represent activities that are not important, even though quadrant three activities are also urgent.

How do you increase your time spent on important, non-urgent (quadrant two) items? Later I discuss multi-tasking, but sometimes you need to stop all interruptions and focus to accomplish your objective. That could mean leaving an entire block of time free from meetings and other commitments. Or, it could mean not taking calls or checking e-mails until you have finished a memo or completed a task. Taking calls and e-mails interrupts your workflow and forces you into a reactive mode—in which you are responding to others rather than maintaining your focus on your own project at hand. It puts you into quadrant three rather than quadrant two. I find it is harder than it sounds to discipline yourself not to take calls and be interrupted, but the payoff of completing your objective in a more efficient fashion is ample reward.

Another key to maintaining your sanity is to expect change and be prepared for it.

Your ability to accomplish a great deal is dependent on your ability to prioritize competing demands. And your ability to maintain your sanity is dependent on your ability to recognize that when something is neither urgent nor important, it may not need to get done—or it may not need to be done by you. Delegate smartly at home and at work. That requires trusting others and letting go. It is an incredibly freeing feeling to take something off your plate—to cross it off your list. But if it's not important or urgent, don't just push it onto someone else; get rid of it for everyone. There's enough work to go around without wasting time.

Another key to maintaining your sanity is to expect change and be prepared for it. Things change minute to minute, at home and in business, so you need to react quickly and calmly. Sometimes in our quest to do it all, we are so tightly scheduled that small changes seem disproportionately disruptive. Recognize that re-prioritizing and adjusting quickly are part of the game. And, as Richard Carlson counsels in his books, don't sweat the small stuff.

As a side point, being late is neither professional nor polite, and it's a hazard of not scheduling your time realistically. When you are punctual, you convey that you are in control and together and respectful of others' time. Leave yourself room to prepare for and get to meetings. Again, as a confirmed maximizer, it pains me to admit it, but arriving five minutes early is better than five minutes late. And, if you are early, you can use that time to reprioritize your day and get organized.

Another facet of managing your time effectively is to be realistic about time requirements. It's hard for me to say this and I truly hate to admit it, but nothing takes five minutes. If you are too aggressive in allocating time, then you will pay the price through either your own extended work hours or sloppy work. Colleen Barrett learned to schedule realistically as executive assistant to Herb Kelleher. For example, she learned in scheduling Herb's day to allow extra time in meetings in which the participants had a strong rapport. If Herb said one hour, then she'd schedule two. Now, it may take a while to see Colleen, but that's because she plans her own time realistically.

LEARN TO SAY NO

Learning to say no is a critical form of prioritizing. The momentary guilt that you feel from not taking on an additional responsibility will probably be small compared to the angst that you will experience from overcommitting. That angst will include guilt for the time that you should be spending elsewhere and frustration for the time you are devoting to your new activity. A helpful strategy for evaluating when to say no is to use a meaningful threshold for accepting new responsibilities. Above, we saw that Dr. Freudenberger determines whether he'd want to make a particular commitment if he knew he had only one more year to live. Connie Duckworth thinks to herself, "I could be doing X or spending time with my kids." These are meaningful thresholds.

Saying no gracefully is integral to leaving you and the party you turn down feeling good. Be honest but succinct.

You don't need to go through an entire story of why you can't participate. It is unnecessary, and it may not even sound compelling to someone else, as your priorities may be different. Instead, simply respond that you're flattered to be asked, but it's not right for you at this time, since you are "stretched thin" and couldn't give the activity the attention it deserves. Then, thank the person for thinking of you. That way, she will feel that the "ask" was appropriate and welcome. And she'll appreciate your honesty in not taking on a project to which you can't fully commit. It's possible to say no—if done nicely—and have everyone part feeling fine.

ORGANIZE THROUGH LISTS AND OTHER RESOURCES

Lists are a critical tool for organizing and executing your priorities. Colleen Barrett creates daily lists of tasks that she reviews before going home at night. And she starts the next day by constructing a fresh list. Barrett admits to being so compulsive about lists that if she takes something off the grocery store shelf and it is not on her list, she may write it down and then cross it off. I find that lists help me accomplish those activities that are important but neither urgent nor palatable. When an item is on my list, I am forced to confront it, and my yearning to cross it off trumps any inertia.

You may prefer one master list, or separate lists by time frame or topic. Valerie Salembier keeps long-term, daily, weekday, weekend, and food lists. Cynthia Round's lists include meal plans for the week, flea market items for her country home, clothes for her daughter, career-related items for herself, including books to read and people to meet, and health appointments.

Other tools can assist you in organizing, too. Electronic and conventional datebooks and various software programs with tickler lists can help you maintain your schedule. Even worse than being late for a commitment is to miss it entirely, so record your obligations through a system that works for you.

Lists are a critical tool for organizing and executing your priorities.

MULTITASK TO INCREASE EFFICIENCY

Multitasking has several dimensions that can help you to work efficiently. On one level, you can try to do several things at one time—such as clearing your in-box while you are on hold for a telephone call, scanning industry magazines in a taxi on your way to a meeting, or folding laundry while you arrange your children's play dates for the next day. At appropriate times, completing more than one task simultaneously enables you to operate more efficiently. There are times, however, when it is best simply to focus. For example, I routinely brought my in-box with me to department head meetings at Chicago Children's Museum. After someone pointed out to me that it sent the wrong signal about how I valued the meetings and the comments of others, I stopped. Now, I notice with disapproval when others use that same technique in meetings. Giving only part of your attention conveys that the meeting isn't worth your focus and mitigates its value. Therefore, if you need not attend a meeting or think it can be accomplished more effectively or efficiently, address that point. Then, rather than offending anyone, you will help everyone.

A corollary to multitasking is accomplishing more than one objective with the same action. Betsy Holden combines her interests in spending time with her children and giving back to the community by teaching Sunday school for her kids' classes. Additionally, she and many other moms develop friendships with their kids' friends' families.

Jackie Woods employs three criteria to ensure that her extracurricular and community service activities fit with her corporate objectives as president of Ameritech Ohio: 1) Is the activity or organization synergistic with Ameritech and where Ameritech gives time and money?; 2) Is it something that employees would be proud to have their names associated with?; and 3) Is it fulfilling? Woods supports the Red Cross, for example, because, like your phone service, the Red Cross is always there. And, if there's a disaster, you need communications, so it's a logical tie. Woods also chairs the board of the local science center because it works with technology, as does her company, and provides an educational, fun place for Ameritech Ohio's employees and their families.

ELIMINATE THE GUILT

Eliminating the guilt also will make you more efficient. The less time you spend feeling guilty, the greater time you have available for more productive activities. When you select one action, it may preclude another. Once your choice is made, be comfortable with it, move forward, and know you can change it. Don't spend 20 percent of your time regretting your selection. As you would in the course of business, make the best decision you can with the information you have and the circumstances in which you find yourself. Then move forward to execute to the best of your ability. That advice holds whether you are a corporate titan or the CEO of your household.

Part of eliminating the guilt is throwing out traditional roles and taboos—for both men and women. You don't have to feel guilty about having a career—with or without children. And you don't have to cook the turkey for Thanksgiving. Rose Marie Bravo spent years creating an elaborate Thanksgiving feast to prove to herself, her husband, and his family that she could be the doyenne of domesticity in addition to a successful executive. Now that she realizes she doesn't have to prove herself, she buys a prepared turkey and lets go of the additional pressure she had put on herself.

> *Once your choice is made, be comfortable with it, move forward, and know you can change it.*

Throwing out assumptions regarding traditional roles involves the whole family. Men increasingly are accepting more and more household and family responsibility. Paula Sneed and her husband, who both travel a great deal (she commutes back and forth from her family home in New Jersey to her office at Kraft's Illinois headquarters) try to divide their work and family responsibilities equally. In Betsy Holden's family, too, there is a real sharing of responsibilities and a conscious effort to optimize roles as a family. Instead of defined male and female roles, there are "things that need to get done." Betsy's husband cooks more than she does.

RECOGNIZE THAT PERSONAL SUCCESS IS A TEAM EFFORT

Personal success, like business success, is a team effort. On the personal side, your team often is referred to as your support network. Exactly what is part of that network depends on your own situation and will change over time as you progress through different stages of your life. Barb Allen's support network includes her husband and a live-in nanny/housekeeper. Allen and her husband, who also has a demanding job, chose where to live based upon the realization that they would need live-in help for their family. Kitty D'Alessio, who is not married and has no children, relies on family and life-long friends for her support network. Mary Ann Domuracki's support infrastructure includes her family, her spouse, and a

> ROSE Marie Bravo's husband is a partner in her professional success. He supports her business role and is the primary manager at home. Bravo comments, "The old saying 'Behind every great man there is a great woman' now should be switched."

fabulous nanny. They split household responsibilities evenly. Domuracki notes, "The worst mistake is to assume you can do it all. I need help from family and friends."

TAKE TIME TO RECHARGE

Taking time to recharge when necessary also prevents burnout by giving you that boost you need to refresh,

Kitty D'Alessio

KITTY, BORN IN 1931, was the oldest of four children, all of whom were great friends growing up. Her parents taught the children to be independent and relatively fearless, a lesson that has helped her in both her business and personal life.

After graduation from Upsala College, Kitty began her work in the fashion industry in B. Altman & Co. department store's training program. Next, she worked at NBC television for $1.25 per hour as a junior stylist to the stars. Though she mostly worked on commercials, she considered the job glamorous, demanding, and rewarding.

At NBC, her talents were noticed by clients, and she soon went to work for Norman, Craig & Kummel. There, she learned to use her empathy and instincts as a woman in her approach to advertising. As she gained seniority, her skills were again noted by a client, and she was brought in as president to turn around the maturing Chanel brand. D'Alessio brought in designer Karl Lagerfeld, worked hard, and traveled extensively.

When D'Alessio gave up the presidency of Chanel, with its emphasis on day-to-day operations and travel, she assumed a vice chairman role. Subsequent ventures have included charity work, starting a catalog business with designer Carolyne Roehm, for which she was president and CEO, and serving as president and COO of Natori. D'Alessio, who likes to "reminisce about the future" with friends and family, is single and resides in New York.

reenergize, and keep going. Today's top women business leaders recognize that fact and have adopted many approaches to recharging. They include going to spas, exercising, taking vacations, going sailing, spending time with family, having an afternoon squirreled away in a quiet museum, and spending twenty-four hours at home with the telephones turned off.

I have found comp (or compensation) time to be a highly effective means to recharge for myself and for others. By comp time, I mean a morning off after a grueling stretch of work to sleep in, to get a manicure or haircut, to exercise, or simply to unwind. In order to be effective, however, comp time must be taken right away after the exceptional work. If you defer comp time to use it as part of a longer vacation, the effect is mitigated, as you do not get the psychological, physical, and emotional refreshment that you need when you need it. Comp time is a small investment in yourself or your employees for a substantial return.

Step Back Regularly to
Review Where You Are

Stepping back regularly to review where you are enables you to gain or keep perspective—to make sure that the path you are on is taking you to your desired destination. If you rush down the wrong path, you only get more quickly to a place you don't want to be. Periodically step back from your day-to-day routine and take time to reflect. Reexamine your values, and reexamine your time commitments. Check to make sure they are aligned. Think about how you want to be known or remembered, and live to those values and objectives.

In many instances, when your values and time allocation are out of alignment you will sense it. But not always. That's why it's important to make stepping back a part of your routine. That could be before the new year, on an annual vacation, at the start of each month, or whenever you are so moved. The key is simply to do it. Be reflective, and be honest.

Periodically step back from your day-to-day routine and take time to reflect.

And remember, you are in charge of your destiny. The power is yours to change what isn't working and to embrace what is. Make the choices that are right for you. And recognize that you are making choices for yourself. I don't deserve anyone's sympathy for not "having time" for manicures, regular exercise, and lunch with friends because I choose to allocate my time differently. Instead, I spend time with my family, write, consult, and engage in community service. I do those things because I want to—not because I am forced. If a manicure, regular exercise, or social lunches meant more to me, then I would rearrange my schedule. Recognizing that I have made those choices—and that I have the ability to change them—is healthy and empowering. Therefore, realize that it is great to have all the options—whether to be a full-time mom or a career person or a community volunteer or some combination of those or something else entirely. Choose what is right for you.

Index